# 10 x 52

# 520 MORE!

## Tips, Tools, & Techniques to Maximize Your Youth Ministry

ISBN 0-9663339-1-8

Evans, Paul
Millergren, AL

10 x 52
520 Tips, Tools, and Techniques
To Maximize Your Youth Ministry

Printed in the United States by:
Morris Publishing
3212 East Highway 30
Kearney, NE 68847
1-800-650-7888

# Table of Contents

# Table of Contents

# 10 x 52

Within these pages are 520 more tips, tools, & techniques to help you maximize your ministry. Don't be surprised if a lot of these sound like common sense because they are. We didn't write a book that contained ideas no one could use, but one that is practical. Our goal is to follow the example of Jesus who said "Now that you know these things, you will be blessed if you do them" (John 13:17).

Each idea is followed by a brief description, summary, or way to use it. This information is practical and may or may not fit your specific position at this time in your ministry. That's why you have 520 ideas to choose from. Somethings will hit you right where you are! (probably most of them).

Use these tips to help you get the most out of 10 x 52.

**Tip #1** *Read with a highlighter.* Make a point glow so you won't overlook it. Come back to it again and keep it fresh in your mind.

**Tip #2** *Use the margins.* If you'll notice, the margins are extra wide. If a tip, tool, or technique comes to mind while reading, write it in. If an idea comes to mind on how to apply the tip, scribble it in the margin.

**Tip #3** *Apply.* As you read you might be thinking, "I ought to try that." Yep! But thinking about it isn't the same as doing it. Put the ideas to use. They can't maximize your ministry on the page, but they can if you into practice.

Maximize Your Ministry!

## ONE

# 10 Reasons to Stay in Youth Ministry

1 **For the Sake of the Call.** Moses stood at a burning bush. Abraham set out for an undetermined destination. Jacob wrestled with God. And you corral an unruly group of teenagers.

When God grabs your heart you can't release the grip even if you want to. God's selection process provides few venues of escape (just ask Jonah). Being called doesn't mean we won't ever want to forsake the mission. It proves that deep down we know we are doing exactly what God purposed us to do.

2 **To Lead Teens to a Mature Faith.** At the end of Hebrews 4, the writer ridicules the believers for failing to grow up spiritually. The Father wants His children to mature into adult walkers, not infant crawlers.

When teens enter college or join the work force, an immature faith will crumble under the pressures of life. By helping adolescents develop a firm faith in God through Bible study, prayer, accountability groups and other means before they leave the group, you aid their faithfulness through life.

3 **To Solidify Family Relationships.** Does anyone know what a nucleus family is anymore? The average youth group contains a host of steps. Step-moms and step-dads. Step-brothers and step-sisters. Few children, it seems, travel through life with the same set of parents.

Divorce claims some, and death claims others. Whatever family structure is in place in the lives of those in the group, our aim is to strengthen the existing relationships for the glory of God. Connect with every family and provide training, encouragement, and support regardless of the family background or battle ground.

4 **To Lead Teens to Christ.** Part of the role of youth minister is that of shepherd. We may have many or few sheep in the fold. What we do know is that many more sheep are wandering lost in the hills than are safe in the shelter of God's arms. Staying in ministry assures that more sheep will come to know the true Shepherd.

Youth workers provide a "professional" source to whom teens can bring their friends for spiritual guidance and healing. They know it's your job to tell others about Jesus, so there is less fear in sharing Christ when they know they don't bear the weight alone.

5 **To Strengthen the Future of the Church.** I know, teens are the church of today, not tomorrow. But your teens aren't called elders, and don't have a say in church business meetings. Their presence may be welcome, but how about their voice?

Use the teen years to prepare teens for a future full role of keeping the church strong. Form leadership teams and teach them how to make godly decisions. Help them adopt a mindset that elevates God's will over tradition or personal opinion.

6 **To Equip Teens for Life.** Ephesians 4:12-13 states that God chooses ministers "to prepare God's people for works of service, so that the body of Christ may be built up until we all reach unity in the faith and in the knowledge of the Son of God and become mature, attaining to the whole measure of the fullness of Christ."

Equipping places the needed tools in the hands of those who will do the work—whoever they might be. Use this space to list the tools you know your group needs to develop to make Ephesians 4:12-13 a reality.

**7 To Show Teens that People Do Care.** Pimples, growth spurts, lack of coordination and other adolescent afflictions make it difficult for teens to believe anyone really cares for them.

Demonstrate how you care by saying and showing it. Let teens know verbally that you care. Don't let a class pass without stating it aloud. Show them you care by being there when they need a friend.

**8 To Use Your Gifts.** Grandma didn't give you that polka-dot sweater last Christmas so you could hide it in the church's benevolent closet. God didn't give you a gift to put it under a bushel, so let your gift shine!

How has God gifted you? ______________________

______________________________________________.

You know the old saying: "Use it or lose it!" Isn't there a parable about that?

**9 To Receive the Reward of Seeing Changed Lives.** "I never thought Sue would come to the Lord with her partying lifestyle." God working a miracle through a life in the group is worth staying in ministry for the long haul. One turn around has the power to keep us around for life.

Youth events are great. All night scavenger hunts are fun (for the teens). But a changed life, that's unforgettable.

**10 To Get Paid.** Reread numbers one through nine. Getting paid for that is awesome. Getting paid for what you love to do is even better! Whether your pay comes from being full-time or part-time, it's a blessing.

If you're a volunteer and wonder what I'm talking about, a special thanks to you for doing what God wants without a check attached.

## Two

# 10 Life Changing Moments

1 **Accepting Christ.** Salvation is literally life changing. While other unexpected events may change the life and heart of teen, this change comes because of a decision.

Part of the redemptive process is repentance, which means to change. A change takes place on the inside that expresses itself on the outside. Being born again may call for a change of friends, change of lifestyle, change of speech...change of everything.



2 **Death of a Parent.** No matter how frequently it visits the planet, we never grow comfortable with death. The death of a parent causes a teen to view life from a different angle, and to acknowledge a loss never to be regained. Things that once seemed so important suddenly drop on the priority list. Parental conversations are revisited to count any unfortunate words, or sounds of love. Brevity of life floods the mind. She considers all the things that she wished she'd said when mom was alive. He wishes for one last fishing trip with dad.

3 **Divorce.** Some feel that divorce is worse than death because the person(s) who caused pain is still around. Bitter words fill the air, and weekend visits fill the calendar.

Divorce can change a teen for the good when abuse occurred at home. It can change for the worse when a distorted picture of love takes root.

4 **When Christianity Clicks.** For kids raised in the church Christianity may seem like little more than 10 a.m. on Sunday morning. Most have never felt true remorse for sin. Most live for Christ without doing much wrong, and not doing much right. If somewhere along the way it clicks, changes take place. Prayers switch from lunch's thankfulness to heaven's gratefulness. The Bible transforms from a rule book to a relationship guide. Friends turn from people to souls. Jesus' sacrifice emerges from an irrelevant moment in history to a connection with grace.

5 **The Class' Clown.** When peers laugh at, not with, a teen, things change. Being teased about weight, teeth, clothes, athletic ability, or more are defining moments for most teenagers. Being labeled dork, geek, nerd, airhead, dummy, or any other epitaph contains the power to shape the future. Sticks and stones can break my bones, but names can break the spirit.

6 **Conversion of a Friend.** Witnessing the salvation of a friend helps a teen see the importance of Christ in the life of another. If the teen studied with the friend, an even greater impact is made.

Give teens the tools they need to share Jesus with their friends. Apply the tools provided on page 102 so your group will have some creative ways to share the Savior!

7 **Conflict as a Christian.** "No, I'm not going to be able to go Friday night..." Whether a party, an empty house with the parents out of town, or a movie that promises enough flesh to keep the audience from blinking, teens face pressures that put their faith on the line.

Holding onto the standards of Christ automatically cancels some dates, conversations, and situations. The activities that other kids get involved in without a second thought can become major temptations for Christian teens. They're tempting not just because of fun, but because of the acceptance that comes along with the acts.

Peter could have been talking to teens when he wrote, "They think it strange that you do not plunge with them into the same flood of dissipation, and they heap abuse on you" (I Peter 4:4). Every teen makes life changing choices based on their response to the pressures to conform.

8 **Death of a Friend.** A monument stands at the entrance to my alma-mater. The name of a teen is etched into the gray granite. His portrait hangs just outside the school offices. Those who knew him, still stop and stare in disbelief.

The death of a friend affects a teen so critically because it's not supposed to happen. Most teens see themselves as invincible, almost immortal. Yet, when one of their own dies, mortality becomes personal.

9 **High School Graduation.** Peaks and valleys fill life. At age five you're the oldest kid in preschool. At age six you're at the bottom of the elementary pole. In sixth grade you're on top again, but by seventh you slip back into the big pond of small fish. In the senior year you know you rule the school...then what? College? Where no one knows your name. Work? Where taxes eat up the small check. Graduation is not only a major stepping stone to adulthood, it's a major leap into the unknown.

10 **The Call of Ministry.** The day a teen realizes that God is calling him or her to a life of ministry everything changes. Goals change. Dreams change. Friends change. The blessing that comes from these changes is knowing that the future holds God's exact purpose.

THREE

# 10 Tips to Keep Teens Committed

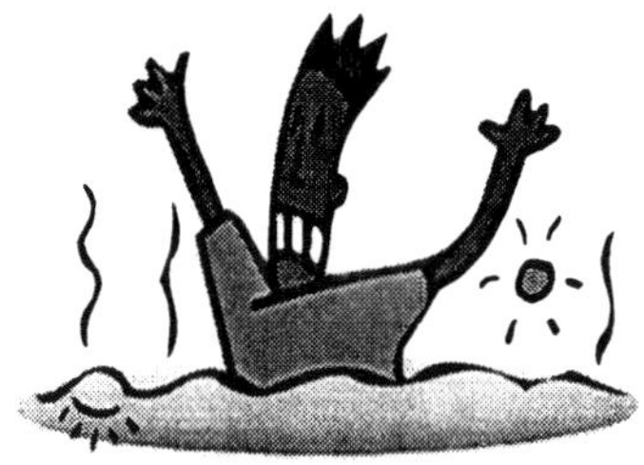

**1 Provide Maturity Classes.** Teens know how to get fed. They plop down in the teen room and wait for you to start talking. But, as you have already discovered, a present body doesn't mean life application will take place.

Teach a seminar or present a class series that will enable teens to feed themselves. Help them develop a daily quiet time and a powerful prayer life. Saddleback Community Church's 201 Class is an excellent resource for ideas. You can reach them at www.pastors.com, or (717)587-9534.



**2 Commitment Contracts.** We are so afraid people might walk away from our ministry that few of us are willing to demand commitment. We act like Jesus formed the "Let's just hang out together" club. He didn't. He formed the "I gave my life for you" club—better known as the church.

You may want to provide varying levels of commitment for your group. Membership demands certain commitments such as attendance and spiritual growth, while leadership may require commitment to leadership growth principles that are tested and evaluated.

Whatever you choose, have each individual sign it so you know they know the standard.

*Commitment Card*

I commit to the following areas as a member of this group:

- Jesus Christ as Lord and Savior of my life.
- Participation in classes and activities provided.
- Daily quiet time
- An authentic Christian lifestyle.

________________________
signature

3 **Regular Spiritual Checkups.** Signing a card doesn't guarantee commitment, so take it a step farther by holding regular spiritual checkups. If your group is small you may be able to meet with one teen at a time and ask about their devotional habits, worship habits, etc.

With a larger group you may want to design a spiritual check up sheet that will allow them to evaluate themselves. I like using the "Spiritual Wheel" (Appendix A, page 167). It's simple but effective. Have the teens grade themselves in different spiritual areas and assign a rating. "1" = poor, "10" = perfect. When they connect the dots, have them circle the high points as strengths, and the low points as weaknesses.

4 **Service Projects.** "Six Flags? Yeah!!!" "Football? You bet!!" "Visit old Mrs. Mathers? Is this a joke?"

Someone said, "You can tell how popular the church is by who comes Sunday morning. You can tell how popular the preacher is by who comes Sunday night. You can tell how popular Jesus is by who comes to the prayer meeting." In our case, you can tell by who comes to the service project. These activities keep kids committed by allowing them to live Jesus, not just talk about Him.



5 **Practice What You Preach.** Jesus told the disciples about the Pharisees, "Do what they say but don't do as they do. For they say and do not." That is an embarrassing statement about the authenticity of the Pharisees. Teens will become more committed when they see you are committed to living, not just saying.

6 **The Nehemiah Principle.** Rick Warren refers to this concept in "The Purpose Driven Church." The key is to repeat your vision every twenty-eight days. Halfway through the rebuilding of the walls of Jerusalem, Nehemiah renewed and reminded the people of the goal.

What is the goal of your group? If a poll was taken of your members, what would they say is the purpose of your group? Write it in the box provided.

If what you have written is what you believe your group

is and should be standing for, then a minimum of once a month recast the vision. Put it on your calendar. Mention it in class. Bring it up at devotionals. Call on a class member to put the vision in his or her own words and tell the class.

7 **Provide Leadership Training.** Use teens who are willing to step up and step out to help forge the commitment of other teens. Meet regularly to equip and evaluate the leaders in your group. You may want to create a newsletter, monthly tape, or a special email-zine to keep the training process on-going. At the very least consider checking out John C. Maxwell's resources at www.injoy.com and sign up for his free monthly email to give you ideas to pass on.

8 **Tie Principles to Action.** Do you remember taking geometry and asking, "When am I ever going to use this stuff?" Teens ask the same thing about our lessons. Keep them committed by following up with an action related to the teaching. For example, if the class study for the week centers on "pure and undefiled religion" as taught in James 1, plan a service project that is orphanage related.



9 **Big Time Believer Buddies.** Purposely put your group around people whose faith amazes you. Expose them constantly to those in your church who are sold out to Christ. Surrounding them with big time believers keeps them committed by showing them that Christianity makes a real difference in the lives of others.

You might take this a step farther and select some adult spiritual leaders to "adopt" different group members to mentor.

10 **Keep Your Guard Up.** All eyes are on you. The youth group wants to know that all they see and hear is for real and making an impact in your life.

As youth workers we have to put a higher standard on ourselves. If Sister Nadine who sits three from the left on the back pew decides to leave the fellowship, chances are good no one in your group will ever know. But if you decide to take a break from God, they may decide to as well.

FOUR

# 10 Techniques for Recharging Your Batteries

1 **Attend A Youth Worker Conference.** Although there are a lot more, here are three conferences that are great:

- National Youth Workers Convention
  NYWC@youthspecialties.com 1-800-776-8008
- National Youth and Children's Ministry Convention
  info@grouppublishing.com 1-800-774-.3838
- National Conference on Youth Ministries 405-475-6314

Use conferences like these and others to revive your spirit of youth ministry.

2 **Retreat.** You take your group on retreats, but how about you? When is the last time you went on a retreat and didn't have to plan it or be responsible for it in any way? When last did you go on a retreat for your personal spiritual growth?

Do some research by calling some friends, or asking some church members about their favorite personal retreat. Or check out www.groupmag.com/pcrc.htm A retreat center to contact for information is The Cove - bgtcreg@thecove.org. 1-800-950-2092

3 **Sabbatical.** Drop back and pull away from your ministry for at least one day a week and one complete week a year. As you know, this term comes from the word Sabbath, which was the day God *commanded* His people to do no work. Although we are no longer bound to the Old Law, the Sabbath principle is biblical. God knows we

function best, thus we can serve Him best, when we've had rest. Don't be ashamed or embarrassed about time off. When most people in the "real world" are off, you are working.

4 **What's Right Club.** Once a month get together with fellow youth workers, friends, family or a combination and have a "what's right" meeting. The key is that you can't complain about anything, you can only talk about what's going right. Share any affirmation, encouragement, positive letters, programming ideas, devotional talks—anything that went right!

5 **Hobby Horsing.** Do you have a hobby? Do you have something you enjoy but don't take too seriously? Hobbies heal us by allowing our minds to remove themselves from the struggles and strains of teenagers' lives and relax in a pastime. Even getting out for a few minutes to enjoy a hobby can recharge the batteries in unexpected ways. So don't feel like a hobby will require a large amount of time (unless you want it to).



6 **Re-read Your Favorite Book.** Write the name of your favorite book. Reading stimulates the brain and forges new creativity. Re-reading a favorite allows you to discover thoughts you missed, remind yourself of thoughts you meant to apply, and allows you to re-enjoy what brought so much joy the first time you read it.

My Favorite Book

7 **Seek Godly Counseling.** No, I did not just call you crazy by suggesting counseling. Don't we all feel better (recharged) when we don't have to keep everything inside? But when do we get a chance to do that? Everyone we talk to is somehow related to our ministry and if we share a struggle, people think we are about to leave, have a secret sin, or are just mean.

What's the answer when you need someone to talk to, but don't feel like you can confide in the flock? Go see someone whose reputation is built on confidence.

Just the thought of it makes me feel better already.

8 **Gimme a Break.** Serious research was conducted and what was discovered is this: Most offices in the United States provide their employees with a ten minute break before lunch, then they receive a lunch break, then they get another ten minute break some time in the afternoon.

We usually work until lunch, take lunch with a church member or eat with teens at school, then return until who knows when. That schedule would wear down that annoying pink bunny. Gimme a break!

9 **Advance Your Education.** Never stop learning to stay fully charged. If you have a degree, work on an advanced degree.

Keep doing what your doing now. Continue to grow from resources that can help expand your ministry.

10 **Walk with the Wise.** "He who walks with the wise will grow wise" (Proverbs 13:20). We all get pumped up when we spend time with people who are able to make us see from different angles. Who do you consider wise? Write three names in the blanks.

1.________________________________
2.________________________________
3.________________________________

Call one of the three this week and set up a time to walk with the wise.

FIVE

# 10 TOOLS FOR TEENS TO USE TO IMPACT THEIR SCHOOLS

1 **Christian Clubs.** Fellowship of Christian Students and Fellowship of Christian Athletes are popular clubs among believers at many schools. If your area schools participate, encourage your group to get involved. If they don't, choose a couple of key leaders and have them approach the school officials with a proposal. They will need to share their ideas about meeting times and places. The president will be responsible for the clubs, and assure the school that it will be entirely student organized.



2 **Locker Love.** Use this tool to spread encouragement in your schools. At one of your meetings give each teen a small sheet of paper that will easily go through a locker slit when folded. Next have them write a general note of encouragement such as, "Have a great day." When they go to school, ask them to distribute the notes in random lockers without adding a signature.

Another option is to contact area businesses for free compact disc coupons or free food coupons to put in the lockers.

3 **Gospel Gear.** Students do notice the Christian messages on t-shirts, caps, bracelets, and other paraphernalia. They also notice the person behind the wardrobe. When choosing gospel gear, arm your teens with two general rules.

1. *Make sure the message and the messenger match.* Don't

wear a heaven shirt and act like a heathen.

2. *Choose positive images.* Clothing or accessories that project an arrogant or know it all attitude impact in a negative way.

4 **Prepare to Share.** So far you've got a group of kids wearing gospel gear, giving locker love, and meeting in Christian clubs. That kind of activity is bound to raise some questions. Prepare your group to "always be ready to give an answer for the hope that is in you" (1 Peter 3:15).

5 **Lunch Bunch.** Designate a certain area for the group to meet for lunch. Use the time to: 1) Talk about victories and defeats of the day so far. 2) Offer encouragement for the rest of the day. 3) Pray for each other. 4) Talk about a passage that will give them strength. 5) Share hurts and struggles. Many teens see their youth group as fun activities with little real life significance. Allow "lunch bunch" to develop into a daily accountability group of sharing and prayer.

6 **Apples of Gold.** This is a teacher appreciation banquet. Host it at your church and have your students invite their teachers to be their honored guests. Fill the evening with entertainment and student testimonies of how their teachers have impacted their lives. You may use music, poetry, skits, or basically anything that will let the teachers know how many lives they have touched.

7 **See You at the Pole** (www.syatp.com). This is the international day of prayer for students held annually on the third Wednesday in September. Students gather around their school's flag pole for a time of prayer. Call 1-817-HIS-PLAN for resources and answers to legal questions regarding this student led event. Resources include brochures, T-shirts, a promotional video, a CD with music and endorsements from Christian recording artists, posters, and other materials.

8 **Breakfast of Champions.** If #5's Lunch Bunch idea won't work well for some in your group, form a breakfast club. Center this meeting pri-

marily on praying for the upcoming day and for specific students. As mentioned earlier, school permission will be required if an on-campus meeting area is chosen.

9 **Thanks for Nothing**. With the risk of their becoming the class un-favorite, ask your group to take their teachers a thank you gift. The key is that there is no holiday or special occasion to justify the gift. When the teacher asks, "What's this for?" teens can reply, "Oh, nothing." Even if the teen who does this becomes unpopular with his/her peers, the teacher will remember it for a long time.

10 **Light and Salt.** "You are the light of the world...you are the salt of the earth..." (Matthew 5:15-16). Challenge your group to become known for holding to a higher standard.

Light shines and penetrates darkness. Our teens should develop a reputation for knowing what's right and what's wrong. Even if others in the school won't follow their example, it's good to know some will decide not to participate simply because someone in your group refuses to participate.

Salt brings flavor to life. After an encounter with teens in your group, people ought to say, "Wow, that was good!"

SIX

# 10 Projects at the Building

1 **Give the Janitor the Day Off.** The custodians of your church know what it's like to feel unappreciated. When the building is clean, it's as it should be, but if anything is out of place, they get the blame.



Honor your cleaning staff with a day off. Assure them that the teens can do a good job cleaning and send them away to enjoy their day.

2 **Adopt a Classroom.** We've all seen the "Adopt-A-Mile" programs put on by highway departments. Do the same with a classroom in your building.

Let the teens choose a room that they will be responsible for. When it needs to be set up for a special event, needs a new coat of paint or needs to some decorating, it will be their job to take care of the details.

3 **Staff Lunch.** Invite the staff to a simple soup and salad lunch. If your staff is small, you may want to use linen tablecloths and china. But regardless of the size add a few personal touches like personal invitations, name cards for seating, hosts, servers, and table clearers. Don't just provide the food and ask them to show up; go all out to provide a true teen dining experience.

4 **Secretary's Aid.** For the secretaries of your church, each week is filled with a thousand and one "to do's." Some tasks only they can do, but some, like stuffing en-

velopes, or taking out the trash, the teens could help with.

Pick out a regular day each week or month for the teens to go to the office after school just to help out. Let the secretary know ahead of time so a list can be prepared of what needs to be done when the teens arrive.

5 **Service Crew.** After services on Sundays the pews are filled with stuff like paper, unused outlines, misused attendance cards, and even Bibles. Get a crew together to comb the pews to throw away the trash, replenish the cards, and collect the Bibles for lost and found.

6 **Wecome Desk Greeter.** If your church has a welcoming area, be sure to get a teen involved. There's nothing wrong with having ancient Mr. Morrow standing there sharing his WWII scars with the guests, but having a teen can add a little life to the situation. Plus it lets visitors know that your church believes its youth are valuable enough to place out front.

You may want to provide a short training course for those who welcome your guests. Make sure they know: 1) Where all the various classes meet. 2) Where the nursery meets. 3) Precise restroom directions. 4) General information about your fellowship.

7 **Clean the Baptistry.** One Thursday night I got a call from a man who wanted to use our building for a baptism. When we arrived the water temperature was perfect. Unfortunately, the five immersed crickets were not.

Avoid the problems of bugs and other things in your baptistry by letting the youth clean it regularly. Ask your janitor about the best way to clean it, and make sure the group knows this is not a swimming party.

8 **Lawn Care.** Get teens involved in the lawn care of the church. There's always plenty to do because weeds and grass keep growing.

Contact the "deacon over lawn" (or whatever the title might be) and give him a list of teens who would like to help. Give him the responsibility of calling the young people who

want to help so it doesn't sound like another lame project you set up for them to do.

9 **Card Copier.** Assign one teen a week to copy the visitor cards and have it ready by the time services are over. Let the church's follow-up ministry know about the service so they can use it to call or email the guests that afternoon, or send a card the next day.

10 **Parking Lot Attendants.** Place a couple of teens at all the entrances to your church so they can welcome people as they arrive. Equip them with signs or knowledge of guest parking so they can send each vehicle in the correct direction.

SEVEN

# 10 Advantages of Small Youth Groups

1 **Everybody Knows Your Name.** "Our name," said Dale Carnegie, "is the most precious sound in any language." A small group holds a strength in this regard. You can look around the room and know each person.



*Cheers*, an old television sitcom, sang, "Where everybody knows your name..." There's comfort and security that comes from knowing others well.

2 **Greater Level of Excellence.** A small group may not have the resources or funds to do everything, but they can do a few things well. Being small can allow for greater focus because there's not as much to distract from the goal.

Use focus as an advantage. State specifically what the outcome should be for an event or spiritual activity, and then put all the ability of the group into that one goal. Pursue excellence through single purpose resolve.

3 **Deeper Relationships.** Not only do teens in a smaller youth group know each other's names, but they have more opportunities to get to know each other on a deeper level. It's tough to be superficial among a few people because there's nowhere to hide. Group members can get to know each other quicker and better by spending more time with a few, rather than less time with many.

4 **You Get to Know the Parents Better.** The smaller the group the easier it is to get close to the parents. You have more time for personal interaction. You seem to be more approachable since there aren't too many people between you and the parents.

Produce as many one on one contacts as you can during a month. It shouldn't feel overwhelming to call, write, or visit each parent with a small group. And, of course, the better you get along with the parents, the smoother your ministry will go.

5 **Less Logistical Problems.** You don't have to tell an intern, "Remind me to call the bus charter place and reserve five buses for this weekend. And, oh yeah, I need to get about a dozen parents to chaperone."

Although you might dream of the day your ministry grows to such extremes, appreciate the ease of keeping up with a handful of kids on one van. It's easier to keep up with them at the mall. It's easier to take care of reservations. It is easier to handle the expense when one teen drops out rather than forty.



6 **Higher Attendance Percentage.** Small youth groups tend to be the community life force. Generally, teens in smaller churches depend more on the youth group for activities and things to do. Thus events have a higher turn out percentage than larger groups.

If you have ten in your group and nine show up that equals 90% attendance. That's awesome! Some large groups are grateful if they can get 40% to show.

7 **Home Devotionals.** Of all the things we did in our youth group, the favorite by far was home devotionals. A family invited the entire youth group over to their house for a brief devotional thought, and for all the snacks we could eat. It was a blast to have the whole group in one place away from the stiff confines of the building. And it was always fun to get to know a hospitable family from the congregation. Try that with a large group and the Fire Marshall has to be invited.

**8 Recognize Visitors Easily.** In a large group a teen may introduce himself to someone who has been a member for five years. A small group can quickly say, "Hey, who's the new kid?"

Visitors will stick out and no one will have to feel embarrassed about wondering if the teen is new or not. Train your teens to make each guest feel welcome by greeting him or her with a smile, and an "It's great to have you here." Use the blessing of a small group to make the most of each moment with a new teen.

**9 Easier Communication.** When it comes to keeping everyone up to date on last minute changes, a small group wins every time. There are fewer calls to make fewer letters to send, and less chance of things being misunderstood.

A small group will allow you to keep the name and number of each teen on you at all times. You may be able to program the entire group into your cell phone for quick calls between meetings or stops.



**10 Know Individual Needs.** A small group offers no place to hide. You know instantly when someone comes to class with a poor attitude, hurt feelings, or tear-filled eyes. While this might seem like a disadvantage to the group, it helps you keep in touch with each individual need of the group.

This may be the greatest advantage of having a small group. A large group can often make you feel out of touch, but a small group can keep you on top of every need.

EIGHT

# 10 Myths of Youth Ministry

1 **All Play and No Work.** Whoever believes this one has never hosted a Junior High Lock-In. As in any ministry, working with youth has many unaccounted hours that the members never see. They see the cookout, but miss the 1 a.m. call from the police station. They see the beach retreat, but miss the flat tire along the way. They see the pizza party, but miss the 10 hour drive back from the work camp.

Tip: Combat this myth by keeping the congregation more informed about mission trips and service projects and less informed on the "fun" activities (since that's all they think you do anyway).



2 **Keeping the Church Informed Will Solve Any Misconceptions.** Don't use this as an excuse to keep people in the dark, but there will be some who think the worst of you and your ministry no matter how hard you try to explain it. Some will think the lock-in is a sex-in. Some will think the contemporary praise is Satan's tool.

Tip: Combat this myth by thoroughly explaining the purpose behind each event.

3 **Working with Christians Is Easy.** Christians can be some of the most unforgiving, harsh, and judgmental people you will ever encounter.

Tip: Combat this myth by being like Christ no

matter how unChrist-like some of the people you work with may seem.

4 **Staff Relations are Fantastic.** Sometimes the staff will seem like a dream, and other times like a drip. Jealousy, gossip, clashing personalities, can quickly grip a staff. One co-worker may feel that another is trying to take over his position. Another may feel that she is being pushed out because of age.

Tip: Combat this myth by putting forth your best effort to make the staff fantastic. Never let it be said of you that you are the one being difficult.

5 **If You are Open and Honest with Teens, They Will Be Open and Honest with You.** You can be as open as an entrance with no door and some kids won't tell you a thing. Instead, they may go behind your back and make fun of your openness.

Tip: Combat this myth by continuing to be open because of the impact it will have on the teen who will choose to open up. Never let the negatives of the few over come the blessing of the many.



6 **If It's Fun They Will Come.** If it's convenient, tailor-made to their liking, and promised to be the greatest event in youth group history, you'll still have no-shows. Fun definitely draws more than boring, but don't count on it to produce a crowd every time.

Tip: Combat this myth by making an event purposeful. Teens are more likely to attend when they know it will be significant to their lives.

7 **A Great Personality and a Great Program is all You Need to Succeed.** Personality and programs are a plus, but even Mr. Dork can build a group with love and acceptance. Personality and programs are things you may be tempted to develop through your own strength and ability. Love and acceptance flow from the Father.

Tip: Combat this myth by refusing to rely on your charisma and ability to generate a first-rate program. Develop a ministry dependant on

God's power, not your cleverness.

8 **When Teens Don't Pay Attention, They Are Not "Getting It."** Teens can act and look like they are a million miles away and then repeat every word you say. They can also refer to a talk you gave a year ago that you can't remember.

Tip: Combat this myth by talking with teens during the week to reinforce whatever you were trying to communicate. They will reveal that they were paying attention, or that they weren't. Either way you get the opportunity to make sure they did "get it."

9 **Teens Prefer Recreation Over Spirituality.** Young people today are looking for a deep walk with God. Years ago teens had very little entertainment outlets so the church scrambled to provide alternatives for teens. Now the whole world seems entertaining, while solid experiences suffer.

Tip: Combat this myth by providing uncompromising lessons and devotionals. Spend quantity and quality time in spiritual activity. Don't be afraid to challenge and convict your group.

10 **If A Young Person Doesn't Come to Christ During Their Teens Years, They Never Will.** While it is true that most people come to Christ when they are adolescents, it doesn't mean they never will if they fail to make a decision during that time.

Tip: Combat this myth by thinking of yourself as a seed sower. Some plants sprout and mature in months, others take years. Keep planting, keep watering, but trust God for the increase.

NINE

# 10 Tips to Spice Up Your Youth Room

1 **Wild Welcome Center.** What is the first thing guests see when they enter your youth room? What impression do you think they receive?

Well, you know what they say, "You never get a second chance to make a first impression." Get a couple of your friendliest teens and station them at the door to warmly welcome visitors. Have a table set up as a welcome area that has resources about your group such as newsletters, class outlines, etc. Also, ask that they fill out a card with their address so you can keep them informed of upcoming events. Hey, while you're at it, offer some light refreshments.



2 **Youth Group Posters.** Most youth rooms adorn their walls with contemporary bands, Christian sayings, and bulletin boards that haven't been changed since 1953.

Be different. Take some photos of your group to a local copy shop and get them blown up to poster size. To take the idea a step further, ask the shop what software they use with their equipment. Find someone in the church who has the same software, scan the pictures, change the background, rearrange the people, and add your own headline.

**3 Themed Décor.** Does your group have a particular name or a verse they love? Why not use it as the theme for your room?

Let's say the group has adopted the sermon on the mount. You could decorate the room with a mountain theme, or maybe even like a jungle. Your praise time could be called Jungle Jams. You could do lessons about Jesus the King of the Jungle. When you have refreshments you can call the sodas Jungle Juice. (Okay, so it's possible to take the theme too far. Just use common sense and make the room fun.)

**4 Logo Logistics.** Use, use, use, use, use, use your logo everywhere. Put it on postcards, visitor cards, posters, letterhead, business cards, apparel, bulletin boards, worship sheets, class outlines, and on anything else your group uses to be seen. You'll know you have reached logo saturation when the church refers to the teens no longer as the "youth group," but by "whatever your logo is."

**5 Media Center.** Parents are constantly worried about what their kids are listening to and watching. Provide a Christ-rated environment. Let the teens donate their favorite Christian artists and movies to the media center and then open it at certain hours during the week for teens to come be together for spiritual music and wholesome videos.



*If you decide to create a media center in your room, don't be cheap. Nobody wants to listen to cd's on a player that skips. No one wants to watch movies on a set that has so much vertical it looks like someone playing with Venetian blinds.*

**6 Crash Corner.** Make your room cozy by setting up house in one corner. Arrange a couple of couches or recliners (love seats may be risky). Create a place to relax before class begins.

If space allows, think about calling one of the soda giants to install a fountain machine. Add a microwave and some popcorn and your crash corner will turn into a smash corner.

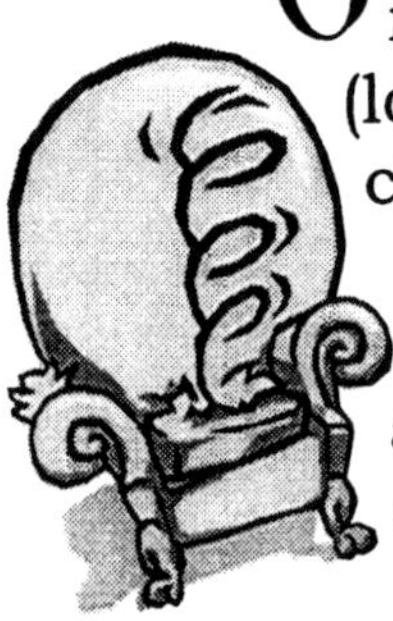

**7 Games.** Religion is such serious business for some that they forget to have fun. Let your teens know fun is on God's agenda by providing games in the room to share your time together. You would be surprised at the number of people willing to donate a foosball or pool table as well as other fun stuff. When people volunteer their board games go ahead and count all the pieces. And as a final precautionary note: stay away from *Twister*, the church leaders never understand how it ties in with fellowship.

> By now you're wondering if you are going to have to meet in a warehouse to do all these things. That's the great thing about this book, use what you can and save what you can't for another time.

**8 Creative Lighting.** Brighten your room with floor lamps, stage lighting, spot lights, black lights, flash lights, candles, Christmas lights, or a combination.

**9 Surprise Set-Ups.** Let your room match the lesson. For example, if you decided to study the Lord's prayer and used Max Lucado's book *The Great House of God* as a reference, you could set up according to the prayer sections. When you talk about the Lord giving us our daily bread, set up the room like a kitchen. You'll get a lot of visitors coming to see your room. And, who knows, they might actually listen to the lesson as well.

**10 Teen Spice.** Get your group together and put them in charge of the entire room. Give them the parameters of what may and may not be done, then get out of the way!

TEN

# 10 Techniques for Fasting

While only one of the fasts in this chapter relates to food they all relate to the soul. Encourage your group to watch for spiritual benefits as they fast.

1 **Food.** Most fasts listed in the Bible use food as the primary target. Why? Food is critical. Without it we get weak. Our stomachs make embarrassing noises. Our moods change.

Before attempting a food fast, contact your physician to make sure you will not have any health complications. Here are three fasts to consider: 1) Junk-food fast. Most teens live off junk-food, so choose a day or a week to stay away from ALL non-nutritious foods. (Tell them that includes pizza.) 2) Juice-only fast. As the title suggests, juice is the only "food" allowed. 3) Water-only fast. This is the most difficult of the three from a physical and mental standpoint. With the first fast you know you're getting healthy food, with the second you know you're getting some carbohydrates, but the third offers no calories. If anyone in the group chooses this fast, encourage them to limit it to a day.

Tip: Tell your group to spend their eating time in Bible Study and/or prayer for a specific request.

2 **Television.** The average young person watches four or more hours of television per day with most of it being spiritually unhealthy. Let the teens know that the fast includes not cheating by taping this week's shows to watch next week.

Tip: A week long fast may provide 28 or more hours to be used for other purposes. Take this fast to another level by assigning daily service projects to be accomplished during television time.

> Choose the length of the fast with the group. With the exception of a juice or water only fast, these fasts can continue indefinitely.

3 **Music.** Do you have any in your group that listen to substandard music? Challenge those members to put up their headphones and CDs and listen to the Lord for a while.

Tip: Offer to keep their music for them during the fast. At the end spend time together examining the lyrics and allow them to make a decision about taking the music back or not.

4 **Loose Language.** This fast includes gossip, suggestive talk, dirty/racial joking, or anything else that would not come out of the mouth of Jesus.

Tip: This needs to become a never ending fast. Form an accountability group named something like *Language Leaners* to forge commitment in this area. Have them meet weekly to discuss their verbal strengths and weaknesses.

5 **Family Blowups.** What if a teen didn't talk back, accepted restriction without arguing, came home on time, and didn't lock herself in her room from after school until the next morning?

Tip: With the teen's permission, meet with the entire family to explain this fast. Encourage the entire family to adopt it for at least a week so everyone will be on the same page and no members will abuse it.

6 **Dating.** For those in the group that feel that they just must have a boyfriend or girlfriend at all times this will be a challenge.

Tip: For those who choose this fast, have them use the time to forge a deeper relationship with Jesus. Look for Bible study resources about Christ and give them to the teens to use during this fast.

**7 Shopping**. From this thing to that thing to everything some kids have to have the best of all that's on the shelves or racks.

Tip: Pinpoint those in your group that focus on the material and ask them to take on this fast for a month. During the month have them write down everything they wanted to purchase and review the list at the end of the month to see what was needed and what was wanted. Take this fast to the next level by totaling the amount of money that would have been spent on material items and collect the money for a charity.

**8 Hobby.** Motorcycle riding, golfing, playing baseball, swimming, etc. This fast is especially good for those who work hard at their hobbies. They may discover that they spend more time working on their backstroke than on their relationship with God.

Tip: Replace the hobby during this fast with their favorite spiritual activity (singing, listening to Christian music, one on one devotionals, etc.).



**9 Internet.** Take a poll of your group and find out how many have online access (100%?). For a designated amount of time, have teens cut all access privileges from email to chat rooms.

Tip: If they have the skill, let the group work on an offline website for the group to be uploaded at the end of the fast.

**10 Phone.** Teens might not talk to you or their parents, but they still talk to each other. Several in your group probably have their own phone line at home.

Tip: Challenge the teens to use their "talk time" to make a list of people they usually don't talk with much. Tell them they can only break the fast by contacting the names on their list and getting to know them better.

> At the end of the fast period set aside a time to get together and discuss the results of the fast.
> Ask each teen to express how they were changed spiritually, and what long-term affect the fast will have.

ELEVEN

# 10 Techniques for Reaching Absent Teens

1 **Call.** This is as simple as it gets. When teens miss several meetings and no one contacts them they don't feel like they are important to the group. If you as their leader don't get in touch with them they feel like you don't care. Pick up the phone, punch in those digits, and let them know how much you miss them.



2 **We Miss You Tape.** Write a "we miss you" song to the tune of *We Wish You a Merry Christmas*. Get the youth group to sing it, then mail it to those absent.

You can take this tip to another level by doing one or all of the following. 1) Insert the absent teen's name in the song. This could call for a lot of recording if you have a large absentee list, but it will be worth it. 2) After the song have different teens encourage him or her to return. 3) If the teen is old enough to drive get permission from her parents to put the cassette in her car so it will start playing when she turns the key.

3 **Monthly Birthday Parties.** Teens might miss church, but they are not likely to miss a party - especially one held in their honor. Send out party invitations to the birthday boys and girls and have teens in the group follow up to make sure they are going to attend the party. Make it a special night where all the attention is on the honoree.

4 **We Miss You Party.** So they didn't come to their own birthday party? What if you held a party at their house? What if you decorated? What if they arrive home with no

clue and find the entire youth group there? What if everyone sang the "We Miss You" song? What if...

This is the type of outreach that can break down every barrier, but here is a word of caution. Use this technique with those who need minimal encouragement to return to the group. Why? Because those who are hard to reach probably have hard feelings and have left for specific reasons that can't be overcome with a party. However, for those who are absent for a general reason such as laziness or light apathy this idea can work wonders.

5 **Digital Postcards.** If you don't already send digital postcards, go to www.google.com and type in "digital postcard." You'll get more sites to surf than you can handle in a millennium.

Some sites will have several varieties of pre-designed cards for you to choose from, or you can design your own. Be sure to personalize it by using the name of the absent teen and including your name. If the service does not let you know if your card was picked up, send another email to the teen to make sure they got your card.



6 **Note Worthy.** Keep detailed records of class attendance and write every teen as soon as possible to let them know they have been missed. Timing is critical. If you wait for six months of absences to accrue, the teens may have made up their minds by then that you don't care about them. After several weeks of sending cards, follow up with a call to discover the specific reason for their failure to return.

7 **Home Visits.** You've made calls, sent notes, thrown parties and they still haven't returned? Try going to their home. Call and make an appointment to drop by and talk for a few minutes. Stay no longer than ten minutes and make it clear how much you miss him or her. Ask if there is anything you can do. Try to determine if there is a spiritual problem or personality tension with another group member.

8 **Teen C.A.R.E.** (Contact, Attention, Relationships, Encouragement.) Teach your teens to C.A.R.E. for each

other.

Have a force of teens that *Contact* anyone who was absent from class or any activity that you keep a regular roll. Concentrate on each teen receiving some sort of positive *Attention* at every event. No teen should come to any function and not have several other teens talk to him or her. Foster strong *Relationships* in your group through whatever means you choose. The goal should be that each teen has at least one close friend in the group that they know they can depend on. Finally, train your group to be *Encouragers* because that's the reason Scripture says we come together in the first place (Hebrews 10:24). What teen would miss a group who C.A.R.E.s?

C.
A.
R.
E.

9 **Teach with Interest.** This may be the area that you can control the most. Make your teaching interesting. Don't let boredom be an absent teen's excuse for dropping out of the group. Get Josh Hunt's book, *Double Your Class in Two Years or Less,* and learn about the importance of presenting a halfway decent lesson.

10 **Don't Give Up.** Hang in there! Keep sending the cards. Keep making the calls and visits. Keep teaching great classes. Keep equipping the teens to C.A.R.E. If a teen stops coming because they gave up on the group - so be it. But if a teen quits because no one reached out to him or her, that's not acceptable. You don't have to spend all your time on absent teens; it would only take a small amount of your weekly schedule to keep in touch.

TWELVE

# 10 Techniques for Creative Email

1 **Half a message.** Who can't send an entire message? Try sending only half the message. In order for the full message to be received have group members respond with a favorite verse or the name of a friend they are inviting to church. End your half message with a teaser that will make them want to respond.

2 **Prayer Tree.** Send an email to one teen with your name at the top and your prayer requests. The person who receives it is to add their name under yours with their requests. They in turn send it to another youth group member who does the same. When the last person with email receives the list they add their name then return it to you. Then you can print it out for meetings or send it to the entire group as a mass email.

3 **Guess Who.** Have your group members turn in a description of themselves to you. Once a week send one out to the group without the person's name. Offer a prize for those who get it right—like getting to sit next to you during church services!

4 **E-Manna.** Once a month email a verse or section of Scripture to the group. Have them write out their

thoughts about the verse then mail you back. Compile all the different thoughts into one message and send it to the entire group so the teens can see what others say about the verses.

5 **Accountability Groups.** Instead of meeting together for accountability have your group e-meet. Have them email each other the same questions to answer each week. Sometimes it's better to write things out rather than talk them out because it allows for a more thoughtful response. Here are five example questions; get together with your group to decide on your own.

1. How would you describe your daily time with God? Why?
2. Who have you shared Christ with this week?
3. What are your prayer requests?
4. How has God worked in your life this week?
5. What sin are you fighting?

6 **Prayer Partners.** Put emails of those who want to participate in a box and let members draw email addresses. Select a night of the week for the prayer partners to share their prayers. Instead of sharing prayer requests have the teens share prayers. Encourage them to type out their prayers to God then email their partner who will do the same for them. This will allow each teen to learn how others pray and it will allow them to pray for their partners more specifically.



7 **Email Scavenger Hunt.** Each person works on their own to complete the list of items required. The rules are that each teen must retrieve the information from friends and group members. The name and email address of the person the information came from must be provided.

For example:

1) Favorite verse from another teen.
   John 3:16; Amy Barnett, abnett@tn.com
2) A quote from a book written between 1920-1960.
   "The days are long like the grass of spring" from Spring Days, pg 134, 1953; Jon Howler, jh@r.com

Make your own list of about 10 items.

8 **Bible Study.** Scan a teen Bible study from a popular series and email it to the group for them to study during the week.

Another idea is to follow up your Sunday study with ways for the group to apply it during the week, or to see how they applied it. If your study had been on 1 John 1:1-4 ask the group to share the ways they heard and saw God during the week. Use this technique to discover good ways truth becomes real in the lives of your group.

9 **E-hell.** We don't spend much time talking or thinking about hell. Part of the reason is because the saved won't be affected by it. Another reason might be that we are terrified of it and want to pretend it doesn't exist.

Get the teens to form the right concepts about hell by helping them understand the passages on the dark world. Select ten passages that speak about hell and email the first one to the group. Supply a couple of questions for them to respond to and write back with their thoughts on the subject. Let them know that you will not send the next passage until you get their response. With the last passage challenge them to list the names of their friends that are lost and to start reaching out to them.

10 **E-Code.** This might be childish for some in your group but you would be amazed at the number of teens interested in an old fashioned decoder project.

You can make up a complex code if you want, or you can do a simple alphabet number code like 1=a, 2=b, etc. Send the message with the decoding instructions. The first teen to decode and email you back wins a prize—like getting to sit next to you in church.

THIRTEEN

# 10 Tips for Teens to Win Their Parents' Hearts

1 **Say and Show.** I John 3:18, "Brother let us love not only with word and tongue, but in deed and in truth." Just like teens, parents want to hear, "I love you." They want to know that their kids care for them. But words alone are not enough. Parents also want to see their child's love for them. 

What could the teens do on a daily basis to say and show their love for their parents? In class or at a devotional challenge the group with that question. In a later class ask for volunteers to share how their "say and show" is going, and to tell about the impact it is having in their homes.

2 **"Yes."** So many kids today do opposite of what their parents ask. Imagine how a parent would feel if a teen simply said, "Yes, Sir" to a request. Having just mentioned say and show, think about John 14:15 where Jesus said, "If you love me you will do what I say." Help your group see how not making the home a battle ground for authority can touch their parents' hearts and change their family relationships.

3 **"Thank you."** Provide paper, envelopes, and writing tools for your group and have them complete the phrase,

"I thank you for..." Without a time limit let your young people write a thank you letter to their parents that is open and expressive. Tell them to thank their parents for the smallest actions to the greatest.

4 **Unexpected Phone Calls.** "Mom, can you come pick me up?" "I need some money." "Can you take me and Kate to the mall after school?" "I'm feeling sick, I need to check out." "I just called to tell you I love you and was thinking about you."

Quick Quiz: Which of the above statements seemed odd for a teen? Can you see the smile and shock on the face of the parent who receives a "I just called to tell you..."? Mom will probably spend the afternoon on the phone calling her friends to brag about the strange behavior.

5 **Help.** Keeping a clean room, doing the dishes, taking out the trash, dusting and vacuuming all are normal teen chores. But a chore means the task has been assigned and is usually unwanted. Teach teens to be helpful on their own initiative. Instead of having a chore attitude, help them develop a *more* attitude where they are willing to do more than expected. That sounds similar to Jesus' teaching of going the extra mile, doesn't it?

6 **Brag on Them.** "Dad, just drop me off at the corner." The message is clear to a parent, "There's a huge risk of you embarrassing me, so drop me off and get out of here." Get teens to put Ephesians 6:1 into practice by honoring their parents by being proud of them. Tell teens to brag on their parents to their friends and teachers. Have them look for honorable qualities in their folks and then reveal them to others.

7 **Dinner and a Movie.** Design a "Dinner and a Movie" coupon to give to the group. Each teen takes the coupon to their parents. It must be redeemed within one month. The offer is good for dinner at a parent chosen restaurant (paid for by the teen, of course), and a

| This Coupon Is Good for One Night Out On Me for Free!! |
|---|

rented movie which the family will all watch together.

8 **Birthdays and Anniversaries.** On birthdays teens could serenade their parents with a lovely rendition of *Happy Birthday*. Or they could make up a song like *You're Not as Old as You Feel* to begin the day with a laugh. It's not so important what the teens do as much as they show that they remembered an important day.

Because of the number of single parent families, anniversaries do not have to relate to marriage. Teens could celebrate the anniversary of their parents' employment tenure, or their sobriety, or their rebirth by Christ.

9 **Massive Mother's and Father's Day.** Moms know they'll get a sweet card from their kids on Mother's Day. Dads know they'll get a tacky tie on Father's Day. Forget the typical; make these days blowouts. Have a planning party and let kids brainstorm together on how to make these days super special. They could decorate the house during the night, cook breakfast and serve it in bed, buy a "World's Greatest Dad!" t-shirt in place of the tie - there are just so many possibilities.



10 **Forgive Them.** Like everyone else, parents make mistakes. Unfortunately, like everyone else, teens can be unforgiving. Remind the youth group of their forgiveness in Christ. Remind them that nothing they have ever done, or will ever do, can take them beyond God's forgiveness. Remind them that forgiveness is the greatest gift a person could ever receive or give.

FOURTEEN

# 10 Tips for Reaching Fringe Teens

1 **Discover Their Fringe.** Each teen lives on a different edge. Some never integrate into the group because of low esteem, drugs, lack of faith, and a host of other fringe areas. Discovering what edge it is a teen lives on, provides a powerful tool in reaching the young person. It doesn't mean that you will necessarily relate to the teen, but you may know someone who has struggled through a similar situation or circumstance who could impact the life of the teen.



2 **Agape.** Love without strings is a rare commodity, yet Jesus shared it without reservations. Though it will not reach every kid, agape love can touch the toughest heart.

Who are your fringe teens? Take out several sheets of paper and place one name at the top of each page. How can you show agape love? Write the answer to that question under the name of each person you listed. Each teen may need a different expression of love, but they will all need it unconditionally.

3 **Walk on Their Fringe.** It's easy to call a teen into an office or make them meet you on your terms. There are occasions for that, but some teens may require that you meet them on their terms and on their fringe. If you have discovered the reason some of the group are on the fringe, go out and meet them there. Get to know them

outside the walls of a class; outside the smiles of a praise song; outside the "church" so all masks can be taken off and the real person can feel free to share their heart.

4 **Social Events.** Some kids on the fringe are not wrestling with some dark secret. Some are just shy and are afraid to get to know others in the group. Get your leaders together and target a fringe kid for your next event. Make sure that the teen will go home knowing that he or she made friends that day.

One thing you might consider is an offsite event like a Christian concert. It will provide drive time which puts everyone in close quarters - and it provides release time where everyone can be themselves without structure.

5 **Errand Impact.** When you're out getting some things done around town pickup a consistent teen and a fringe teen and take them with you. Use the drive time to let both teens get to know you better, but especially the one that's not involved.

Teens can develop the idea that ministers live in some strange spiritual world of perfection that they don't live in. This tip will help them see you as a real person.



6 **Remember the Past.** I bought the wrong daily calendar for this year. In October I went to buy a refill and saw a great deal and snatched it up. No wonder it was a great deal, it was a get "rid of this year's calendar" sale. On January 3rd I realized the mistake. I was living in the past.

The past isn't all that bad to remember when it can help you in the present. Do you remember not fitting in? Can you recall a time when you were a fringe kid? Use those experiences to reach inactive teens.

7 **Mentoring.** This term and discipling get a lot of press with good reason. Lives are changed more radically and more permanently through the aid of someone leading the way.

Jesus discipled, mentored, the twelve. He spent time with them and showed them how to live. Fringe kids need the same. What adult can be a living, breathing Jesus to a teen on the edge?

8 **Core Outreach.** Who are the teens you know you can depend on? ________________________________________

________________________________________________________.

Equip those teens with the tools needed to reach the teens who don't want to be reached. Share some of the previous examples with them. Brainstorm and make a list of ways to reach out. Assign a teen to each of them and tell them to make one phone call and send one letter a month to their teen.

9 **Don't Force It.** "Aw, com'on. You know you want to get involved. It will be so much fun. You haven't come to anything in a looooooong time. I talked to your mom. She really wants you to get involved. She says it will be a good thing for you. Com'on we'll have a great time. I tell you what. If you don't have a fabulous time you can shave my head in front of the group. How about it? Doesn't that sound like a blast? Okay, I'm going to give you one more chance to accept this one time offer. Going...going... going..." They're gone.



10 **Lower Your Expectations.** If a fringe teen decides to start attending regularly don't expect him or her to conform to the image of the group. Your group may be clean-cut and proper, while the new arrival may be uncut and rude. Don't be concerned about their conforming on the outside, but the transforming on the inside (Romans 12:2).

> Never stop reaching for the teen on the edge of the group. As long as your hand is extended, it's their choice whether or not to participate.

FIFTEEN

# 10 CAUSES FOR TEEN ALCOHOLISM

1 **Experimentation.** We all have a little Indiana Jones within us. We want to make a discovery. We want to step into the unknown to find out what it holds.

The lure of the unknown draws many kids to drink. What will it be like? What will the buzz feel like? How much can I handle? What's all the fuss about? So with a mind full of questions and only one way to discover the answers, they experiment.

Tip: Don't just tell the teens not to drink. Tell them why. Answer the questions they have.

2 **Peer Pressure.** What kid can withstand the urging of a friend, "Don't be a sissy, just try it." The need for acceptance can override every rational thought and decision.

Tip: Prepare the group by giving them a list of phrases that may be used to get them to drink by their peers. With the group, decide on some Christian comebacks for the situations.

3 **Family Stress.** There used to be a commercial where a lady stood in the middle of her kitchen with the world spinning frantically around her. She escaped all her troubles by slipping into a warm bath. Some teens use liquor as their warm bath to escape their family problems.

Tip: Help teens see that hiding from a problem through a can of beer or a shot of vodka will not make the problem disappear.

4 **Parent's Example.** When a parent drinks and alcohol is in the home chances are good that a child will either think it's no big deal, or they will sneak a few swallows here or there. The problem with a few swallows is that it can turn into dependency.

Tip: Try talking to the parents about the temptation given by having drinks available at home.

5 **Media Messages.** The most clever commercials have to be beer commercials. They make frogs talk and beautiful babes surround average guys.

Tip: Tell teens the commercials are true. Under the influence of alcohol animals talk, ugly girls look good, dorky guys become hunks, and driving a car is like riding a roller coaster - until the sudden stop and loss of life.

6 **Relationships.** In a similar way to #2, teens use alcohol to escape relationship problems. A break-up with a boyfriend or girlfriend may bring on a binge. An absence of friends may cause a young person to make a friend of the bottle. Desertion by someone a teen thought they were close to may trigger the thought of drink.



Tip: Get some, "Don't Hide, Confide" cards printed with your name and a variety of contact numbers so you can be reached 24/7. Assure teens that you are serous about them calling you at any hour when they feel like drinking.

7 **School Struggles.** Low academics, failure to make a sports team, or a list of other daily derisions at school can make a teen want alcohol for comfort. What are the most common school struggles that your teens face? How many in your group employ alcohol as a way to cope?

Tip: Cope and comfort are key words. Approach teens who are having a particularly difficult time at school and offer your time and ears. Most teens don't want to admit they have a problem. It's embarrassing and it makes them feel weak. Let them know you will not judge, only listen.

**8 Low-Self Esteem.** Drinking not only holds the power of making someone homely look good. Its delusional affect can make an insecure person feel invincible. Ninety-eight pound weaklings will take on a hulk under the influence.

Tip: As suggested in 10 X 50, help teens develop God-esteem. Let them know that God has bought them with a price and that they are priceless to Him. Because of this God wants all His children to use, not abuse, their bodies (I Corinthians 6:19-20).

**9 "Too Cool."** While some teens are insecure others are so arrogant that they use liquor to flaunt their superiority. They brag about how much they can drink and how they can get as much alcohol from their "source" as they want. They talk about drinking with their parents. They throw wild parties and are obnoxious.

Tip: Take extra caution when dealing with the cool. Their pride can cause them to walk away without listening. Challenge them to have the spirit of Christ who came to serve, not to be served (Mark 10:45).

**10 Misplaced Priorities.** When God is not at the top of life's list alcohol is an easy replacement. Without the purpose and direction provided by a relationship with the Almighty young people get quickly disillusioned.

Tip: Keep doing what you are doing. Stay faithful to Christ and to the kids even in the middle of their struggles. Never turn away, but always toward them to show how Christ's love has transformed your life. Never give up on a teen.

## SIXTEEN

# 10 Tips to Teach Teens About Worship

1 **Let Your Love Shine.** "Love the Lord your God with all your heart and with all your soul and with all your mind and with all your strength" (Mark 12:30).

Worship expresses our heart to God. Words may be difficult to find, or feel inadequate, so let teens know that the heart's words are what matter most to God.

2 **Get Close to Him.** "Let us draw near to God with a sincere heart in full assurance of faith..." (Hebrews 10:22).

Children crawl up in the lap of their parents knowing they will be accepted. God invites us to enter the lap of His love with confidence. Sincere hearts of worship allow all believers to get close to the Father.

3 **Encourage Each Other.** "Let the word of Christ dwell in you richly as you teach and admonish one another with all wisdom, and as you sing psalms, hymns and spiritual songs with gratitude in your hearts to God." (Colossians 3:16).

During our corporate worship times it's tempting to get so focused on the Lord that we forget those around us. God reminds us in this passage that our songs to Him also bless others. We sing with gratitude to God, while we sing with purpose to each other.

4. **Witness Worship.** "In the year that King Uzziah died, I saw the Lord seated on a throne, high and exalted, and the train of his robe filled the temple. 2Above him were seraphs, each with six wings: With two wings they covered their faces, with two they covered their feet, and with two they were flying. 3And they were calling to one another: "Holy, holy, holy is the LORD Almighty; the whole earth is full of his glory" (Isaiah 6:1-3).

It's tough to do what you have never seen. Whatever concept of worship Isaiah conjured before this encounter must have been blown away. Encourage teens to watch other worshipers during the service. Let them witness another's heart rise to God.

5. **Worship Creates Hunger.** "As the deer pants for streams of water, so my soul pants for you, O God. My soul thirsts for God, for the living God. When can I go and meet with God?" (Psalm 42:1-2).

When is the last time you heard a teen say, "When can I go and meet with God?" When you hear that phrase you know you've met a worshiper. Entering the Lord's presence through worship creates satisfaction and hunger simultaneously.

6. **Raise Your Praise.** "Clap your hands, all you nations; shout to God with cries of joy. How awesome is the LORD Most High, the great King over all the earth!" (Psalm 47:1).

In the blank provided write the name of the last professional football event that you attended that was quiet: _________________________. Is the blank still blank? Do you know why? Because the people in the stands are worshipping what's happening on the field (at least one group of fans). When God is active in our field of life we respond with praise.

7. **Let God Find You.** "Yet a time is coming and has now come when the true worshipers will worship the Father in spirit and truth, for they are the kind of worshipers the Father seeks" (John 4:23).

God is looking for us. He is seeking us. Will He

find us? If we had a special pair of glasses that revealed true worshipers, how many people would be in the pews Sunday morning? How many would God find?

8 **Express Your Experience.** "Then Moses and the Israelites sang this song to the LORD: 'I will sing to the LORD, for he is highly exalted. The horse and its rider he has hurled into the sea'" (Exodus 15:1).

Yep, the man who complained to God about his lack of speaking ability is leading a congregation of 1.5 million in worship. If Moses can sing a new song to God, so can teens. When the Lord delivers them or strengthens them, tell them not to hesitate, but to lift God up on the spot.

9 **Christ is Present.** "For where two or three come together in my name, there am I with them" (Matthew 18:20).

It's amazing the number of times we worship as if God is nowhere around. But He makes it clear that He's not only around, He's in the middle of the praise.

10 **Never Stop.** "And they stayed continually at the temple, praising God" (Luke 24:53).

Worship is not an hour on Sunday morning, Sunday night and Wednesday night. Worship is anything that brings glory and honor to God. Develop your group into full time worshipers. Change their focus from set aside periods of worship to a lifestyle of worship.

SEVENTEEN

# 10 Techniques for Making the Elderly Feel Special

1 **Give a Warm Greeting.** Just like teens, older people want love and acceptance. Yet, because of the generation gap and other differences, ignoring them often results since "They're not in my ministry." Look around your auditorium on Sunday. What percentage of your congregation is older?

Lay down any excuses and hold out the hand of hello. Share a smile. Ask how they are doing. Show that you are interested in their lives.

2 **Adopt a Grandparent.** Divide the teens into sections of five and let each group select one older member of your church to adopt. Their responsibility will be to call and check on them once a week and to invite them join their family for lunch once a quarter.

3 **Visit.** A lot of the elderly spend their days alone and silent. As you run errands during the week, or on your way back from lunch, stop by and visit a shut-in. Tell them about youth work and let them tell you about their family or anything else they desire.

Visits don't have to be long to be productive and remembered. Though some of the elderly might like it if you stayed all day most will appreciate that you thought enough of them to stop and talk.

**4 Senior Survey.** Get a list of the members of your church that are above seventy years old and send a survey. Some items you might want to include are: 1. What are the greatest concerns of the older members of our congregation? 2. Would you like for teens to come over occasionally to help you with house or yard work? 3. What is the most important thing you have learned in your lifetime?

The questions don't have to be deep, but try to do two things. First, they should allow the person to tell about him or herself. Second, they should deliver useful information that can be used by the teens for service.

**5 Shopping Trips.** Ask the secretary for the names of elderly members who are not able to drive, but who are able to get out of their homes. Select a Saturday, get the youth group and the church van or as many cars as you need and take them shopping. Let them know exactly when you will pick them up and when they can expect to return home. Assign a teen to each one to spend time with them at the mall or shopping center.



**6 Group Singing.** Dust off the song books, load up the van and head to an older person's home to let the vocals rip. The elderly say they enjoy this format because it reminds them of the churches they attended when they were young. Take requests and sing as many songs as time allows.

Don't be afraid to teach new songs. Bridge the generation gap by explaining that today's contemporary music connects with today's young person the way a favorite hymn connects with the person you are visiting.

**7 Read Aloud.** Perhaps you have some members whose age has affected their eyesight to the point of not being able to read. All you will need to show you care is a Bible and your voice.

You may want to call ahead to ask about any special passage the person would like read, or if there is a special book they would enjoy a few chapters from. Maybe they would enjoy a couple of excerpts from 10 X 52—then again, maybe not.

8 **Spring Cleaning and Rearranging.** Some of your more frail older members may enjoy a different look to their home setup. Offer to bring the teens over to rearrange the furniture and throw anything out that is no longer needed. Don't try to talk them into anything. Follow their directions exactly as they orchestrate.

9 **Church Pickup.** My Grandmother lives in a retirement apartment and the church she attends sends a mini-bus over to pick her up for every service. She loves it because she is not able to drive herself and the church is too far for her to walk to services.

Even if your church already offers this transportation, offer to run the route once every couple of months and take some teens along. Assure the elderly that the teens won't be driving and everything should work out fine.

10 **Gift Baskets.** It's an old and possibly overused idea, but only because it's a good idea. Fill a basket with notes of encouragement and easy to eat fruit or candy, and deliver it with a homemade card that lets them know how much the youth of the congregation appreciate the elderly of the congregation.

EIGHTEEN

# 10 Tips for Recognizing Teen Depression

**1 Appearance.** In some teens depression will produce ongoing sorrow with a look of ongoing hopelessness. Their skin tone can lose its healthy color. Some appear frail and weakened by their depression.

Tip: Ask about their life. Their appearance could be attributed to a relationship breakup.

**2 Eating Disorders.** Overeating, anorexia, and bulimia can all result from depression. They are all coping mechanisms. When a teen is depressed about their appearance any of these could result.

Tip: If anyone in the group is acting abnormally down or continually complains about his or her body, casually watch their eating patterns. Do they gorge? Do they always rush to the restroom after a meal?

**3 Insomnia.** This is not lack of sleep, but the inability to sleep. A teen's melancholy may keep them awake. They want to sleep, they need their rest, but it won't come.

Tip: When you hear a teen talk about not being able to sleep ask about how long it has gone on. If it's just a couple of nights then ask again in a few days. If it's been months investigate further.

**4 Lack of Concentration.** Do any teens drift into their own world? No, not during your classes. Do you notice the inability to focus regardless of the situation? Depression can take you miles away from reality. Everything is filtered through the lens of doubt and insecurity.

**While these are some common symptoms of depression don't get paranoid. Many of these will overlap if depression is the true problem.**

The tendency is for the lack of focus to show up as apathy. The teen doesn't care what the group does. It doesn't matter where or when an event takes place. Nothing seems to matter because all that can be seen clearly and focused on is the sorrow at hand.

Tip: Give a specific task for the teen to focus on for a short amount time. Help them increase their ability to concentrate.

5 **Suicidal Thoughts.** Severe cases of depression bring on thoughts of taking one's life. It feels as if there is nothing to live for. Nothing holds significance under the fog of depression.

Because of the intense hopelessness, teens may think their families, friends, the world as a whole would be better off without them. They may think that since their emotional downs affect them so greatly they must have the same effects on others.



Tip: When teens start mentioning suicidal terms watch for other characteristics like those listed on page 96.

6 **No Vision.** Talk to a teen struggling with this problem and they will tell you about a bleak future with no light at the end of the tunnel. They have no vision for their lives. They believe others can and will succeed, but their life is doomed to sub-mediocrity.

Tip: Don't go overboard with this, but do reveal some aspects of their lives that hold promise. They may not believe you at the time, but when they are in an up mode they will remember your encouragement.

7 **Extreme Weight Loss.** While some teens overeat when they are depressed, others choose to under eat. They may blame their weight for the feelings they have and

choose to "diet" to change their appearance and thus change their mood. They don't realize that a large portion of their negative self-image has been created by their negative mental state.

Tip: When weight loss is sudden and dramatic make sure their parents have noticed the problem as well. Busy moms and dads can miss glaring signs of a problem and are quick to accept a teen's excuse.

8 **No Energy.** I spoke with a young lady last week who said, "I don't want to get out of bed. I don't want to go to school or the mall. I don't even want to turn the lights on, I just want to sleep." Some depressed teens feel tired all the time. Caffeine or calories make no difference. All they want to do is sleep, which of course, allows them to escape their struggle.

Tip: Ask if they need you to call them before church or a youth event to make sure they are up and on their way. If that's not enough let them know what time you will be by to pick them up.



9 **Strong Feelings of Guilt.** Depression magnifies negative feelings of anger, sorrow, and guilt. It can cause a teen to remember a sin from several years ago and renew the guilt as if it just occurred.

Tip: Remind teens that forgiveness is forever. We have God's promise that He will always forgive us (I John 1:9).

10 **Overly Sensitive.** This is a no brainer. Kids that used to be able to dish it out and take it as well are no longer able to endure the casual teasing. They take it personally and use it to feed the insecurity brought on by their depression.

Tip: Be sensitive to the sensitive and pass the same advice on to the group. An easy target gets more of the rough comments than a person who doesn't care. Be protective of teens whose sensitivity is a direct result of depression.

NINETEEN

# 10 Tools for New Member Initiation

1 **Invisible Obstacle Course.** Send all your new members to a back room and bring them out one at a time. Stand them in front of an obstacle course of paper cups, plastic soda containers and other non-lethal objects that can be stepped over. Have group members stand on both sides of the course to mark the boundaries. Instruct the new teen to take a careful look at the course memorizing it in his mind. Next blindfold him and tell him to listen carefully to the instructions group members will be yelling to help him make it through the course. As the group begins to yell conflicting directions, have the group reach in quickly and remove all obstacles. They will continue to tell the new teen to "Jump", or "Take one large step forward", or "Be careful you almost stepped on a cup!" After he completes the non-existent course take off his blind fold and show him what he meticulously maneuvered through.



2 **Chubby Bunny.** This is an old but fun game. Line teens up facing their peers. Walk to the first with a large bag of marshmallows and tell her to chose one and place it in her mouth repeating the phrase, "Chubby bunny." Repeat this process with each teen over and over again until none can say "Chubby bunny," or until the marshmallows must be spit out. Be sure to have a waste basket or plastic bags available for quick marshmallow mouth de-

posit.

3 **Embarrassing Photos and Videos.** Talk with the new members' parents and get them to give you any incriminating materials from childhood. Goofy Easter pictures or live video performances from age two. Use these items to let the group learn more about their new guys and gals.

4 **"You Light Up My Life."** Get a recording of the song "You Light Up My Life" and run off a set of lyrics for each teen being initiated. Have each one hold a flash light or a candle and sing the song to the rest of the group. If they don't sound sincere enough let them sing it again. Perhaps you have a new kid that really likes to ham it up. Let him or her do a solo to get the shy teens out of the spotlight.

5 **Animal Name Song.** It can be overwhelming to enter a new group and know only a few names, so form a circle and sing the animal song. Get a jungle beat going and the first person begins, "Hi, my name is Jack and I'm a jaguar." Then Jack become a jaguar with actions and sounds. The second person says, "Jack is a jaguar (repeating the actions at the same time). My name is Susan and I'm a spider monkey" You get the idea. Each person repeats all names and actions before them, plus adds their own. No animal may be used twice.



6 **Cornbread Cake Contest.** Yes, it's exactly what it sounds like. Make cornbread in a large cake pan. Whip up some instant mashed potatoes and add some food coloring, this is your icing. Cut a large piece for each new teen. The first one to eat the entire piece gets to go on the next youth trip free! Of course the trick is that you don't tell them it's cornbread, just mention the cake aspect. Have your camera ready for the first bite.

7 **Vow of Commitment.** Line the new folks up and have them repeat after you with their right hand raised. "I have the right to remain silent on all youth trips...I have the right to be back on the van on time at all times...I

have the right to return home early from a trip if so needed..." Write your own, but add some serious points at the end such as, "I have the right to receive unconditional love from each youth group member...I have the right to call (your name) any time of the night or day with a problem..."

8 **Banana Eating Contest.** Pair the new person with a current youth group member and blindfold both of them. The crowd gets to choose who they will cheer for. Place before both contestants cut up banana pieces. As you yell "Go!" the current member rips off his blindfold and replaces a banana wedge every time the new guy puts one in his mouth, while the teens continue to cheer both teens.

9 **Teen Testimonies.** Select several group members to share what the youth group has meant to them. They should share how they have been loved, supported, and challenged.

10 **Induction of Honor.** For those of you who don't want to use any pranks for initiation have a simple banquet. Get some volunteers to cook the food. Seat the new members at a table of honor up front, or on a stage. Have group members write each new teen a note of encouragement to be presented to them during the evening.



Choose your initiation process wisely. You want the new teen to feel welcome, not embarrassed. Use the tools that match the personality of your group.

TWENTY

# 10 Youth Ministry Websites



1 **www.youthpastor.com.** YouthPastor.Com was founded in 1997 to create the most comprehensive youth ministry network and online 'free' resource for youth pastors. YP's focus is dedicated to the youth pastor, designing resources and services that are not typically available from the church's denomination and Christian curriculum publishing services. Instead, their services complement the offerings of specialized ministries and curriculum publishers.

2 **www.youthspecialties.com.** "For 30 years Youth Specialties has worked alongside Christian youth workers of just about every denomination and youth-serving organization. We're here to help you, whether you're brand new to youth ministry or a veteran, whether you're a volunteer or a career youth pastor. Each year we serve more than 100,000 youth workers worldwide through our training Seminars and Conventions, resources, and here on the Internet." (From Youth Specialties *Who We Are* web page.)

3 **www.grouppublishing.com.** From its beginning in 1974, and through all of Group's products and services, Group has encouraged Christian growth through the unique approach of "authentic learning." In the past 25 years, Group has grown to be an organization of more than 200 staff-people who are dedicated to helping children's and

youth workers, Sunday school teachers, Christian education directors, and pastors bring millions of children, teenagers, and adults closer to God.

4 **www.castyournet.com/EGAD!/index.html.** "Sometimes there just aren't enough hours in the week to take care of youth meetings, retreats, board meetings, Sunday services and a myriad of other tasks required of today's youth minister. Perhaps you are a volunteer who ministers to young people on a part-time basis. Whoever you are... EGAD! is here to provide you with hundreds of practical, economical and creative ideas for you to incorporate into your ministry to youth." (from their web page).

5 **www.dougfields.com.** The original Purpose Driven Youth Ministry guru. Doug's site provides information on all his products with a few freebies thrown in for good measure. His creativity and heart for teens shine through all his ideas. Be sure to sign up for his email list. Doug says this about *Making Young Lives Count*, "Making Young Lives Count is the name I chose for this company because I didn't want to call it "Doug Fields' books and tapes and stuff". The title of the company describes what I want to do while I'm alive."



6 **www.sermons.org.** Sermon outlines, stories and illustrations. I know most youth ministers don't like the word preaching or sermon, so think about this as a resource to help make your youth talks strong. The great thing about this site is you can get a lot of lesson ideas and adapt them for your particular ministry. It also serves as a great starter site. That means you can go there and get an idea to get you started that in the end may in no way resemble the original lesson.

> Like everything else in life, the web can be a tool for God's purposes or Satan's purposes. Stay focused while surfing.

7 **www.gospelcom.net/injoy.** INJOY as an organization is dedicated to developing leaders of excellence and integrity by providing the finest

resources and training for personal and professional growth. John Maxwell is known internationally for equipping and training leaders. Some of his materials will enhance your ministry by giving you the tools needed to take your leaders to the next level. Sign up for his monthly newsletter and for the pastor's coach newsletter.

8 **www.crossearch.com.** Over 900 youth ministry resource links are available from this site.

9 **www.uthstuph.com.** "Uth Stuph exists for one reason and that is simply to support ministry. God has given us a vision of providing creative resource tools for ministries. We have fought the battlers, and we understand your mission!

We know you are in the trenches and our goal is to give you the tactical support to make your job easier. Uth Stuph has grown to serve over 2,000 ministries from across the US and Canada. Our mission is simple: to exceed customer expectations." (from their web page). Their design services are creative and affordable.



10 **www.youthministrynow.com.** A site that uses well known youth authorities resources. Articles from Duffy Robbins, Les Christie, Bible studies - updated monthly.

List Your Favorite Websites here and tell a friend about them so he or she can be blessed.

TWENTY ONE

# 10 Must Reads

1 **The Bible.** Have you ever read the Bible from cover to cover, the whole thing and not just your favorite books? Regardless of the number of fresh ideas circulating through the pages of new books this ancient text is our only legitimate guide for life and ministry.

The Bible is not about what God did, but what He does. It is not just about Moses, David, and Daniel - it is very much about us. Our story is contained between the onion skin pages. Before reading or turning to another book for advice and guidance read the Book.



2 **Moments with the Savior.**
Ken Gire, ISBN 0-310-50070-2. This devotional book "delicately weaves events, emotions, thoughts and faces into a moving depiction of the life of Christ." Ken writes in a style that will make you feel that you are taking steps with Christ through His ministry.

3 **Color Outside the Lines.**
Howard G. Hendricks, ISBN 0-8499-1569-4. Subtitled "a revolutionary approach to creative leadership," *Color Outside the Lines* takes you beyond the box most of us live

our lives in. Hendricks provides a nine-step process to unleash your creative spirit.

**4 Back to the Heart of Youth Work.**
Dewey M. Bertolini, ISBN 1-56476-396-X. While many books on youth ministry center on programs, this one centers on the heart. Dewey reminds us that a relationship with God and others sums up youth ministry. This work shows that you don't need gimmicks to have a successful ministry.

**5 The Ministry of Nurture.**
Duffy Robbins, ISBN 0-310-52581-0. Do you ever wonder about ways to build a real life faith in your teens? Duffy offers practical ideas backed by research to show you the why behind the how. Jesus commands us all to make disciples; Duffy's book tells how to do it today.



**6 Public Speaking for Dummies.**
Malcolm Kushner, ISBN 0-7645-5159-0. Don't write a letter, we know this book isn't written from a Christian perspective. What is does hold is invaluable tools to make you a better speaker and class teacher. These 384 pages provide enough for the beginning speaker to veterans. Malcolm covers humor, stage fright, organizing a talk, eye contact, and a whole lot more. Don't let the dummy title fool you, this is smart stuff.

**7 Fresh Wind Fresh Fire.**
Jim Cymbala, ISBN 0-310-21188-3. Through the story of Brooklyn Tabernacle members, Jim Cymbala reveals the power of God. He firmly believes that we don't need more preachers, books, neat doctrinal statements, or anything else. We simply need God. Powerful.

8 **Purpose Driven Youth Ministry.**
Doug Fields, ISBN 0-310-21253-7. Based on the Saddleback Church's ministry format, Doug takes the best and makes it better. He makes it clear about how to build a ministry around the five purposes of the church found in the Great Commandments and the Great Commission. The strength behind this approach is that the mission never becomes cloudy. Every teen in the group can know exactly where the ministry is headed and what is expected of them.

9 **Visioneering.**
Andy Stanley, ISBN 1-57673-538-9. 
"Vision," writes Andy, "is a clear mental picture of what could be, fueled by the conviction that it should be." Visioneering can help you discover and maintain God's unique purpose for your life. Based on the book of Nehemiah, Andy presents teaching and exercises so you can get to the end of your life knowing you have not missed your purpose.

10 **The Message.**
Eugene H. Peterson, ISBN 08910-97287. This New Testament paraphrased in contemporary English is a blessing to read. Peterson takes a text that can feel old or stuffy and brings it to life in today's vernacular. The Message is fun, freeing reading.

# TWENTY TWO

# 10 Techniques to Build Staff Unity

1 **Pray Together.** When the believers prayed together in Acts 4 things got shook up. Shake up your staff by praying together with passion. File the stale prayers. Trash the archaic language. Release your hearts together to the Father.



Select a minimum of one day a week to meet to pray together. One of my most disappointing times in ministry occurred when a staff member said he didn't have time to pray with the rest of the staff.

2 **Develop Openness and Honesty.** With all the eyes that are on you it's easier to form a force shield than transparency. With the risk of others belittling your sincerity it's tempting to build a wall rather than let down your guard. But openness holds more promise than pain when approached correctly. Openness and honesty places everyone in the same boat. Dreams become vivid. Hurts receive healing. Discouragement obtains support.

Start slowly with this technique. Opening the flood gates of your emotions at the first meeting may cause others to feel uncomfortable or scared of what they may have to share. Begin with a no stress exercise like, "What gives you hope?" As the barriers dissolve move toward deeper topics like secret sin or insecurities.

3 **Discuss Your Ministry Needs and Wants.** "You do not have because you do not ask," James 4:2. Do you ever feel alone? Do other staff members know you exist? Even

in the most casual of meetings, mention your ministry. Ask about their ministries and how they are going. Let them know how they could enhance your ministry and tell them that you are available to help them in their area. Do all of this in a non-threatening way. Come across humble, not like you're ready to take over their territory.

4 **Do Your Job.** Peter said that we should always be ready to give an answer for the hope that is within us. We should also be ready to give an answer for the hours of our day. Division advances quickly in a staff member who feels others are not doing their fair amount. Because of your irregular hours make a point to keep the staff informed of your schedule. If you go home around four in the afternoon to spend time with your family, let others know you will be back for a meeting from seven until ten that night.

5 **Brag on Each Other.** Sticky notes are a wonderful tool. Why not use them to encourage your fellow staff members? Leave one on the secretary's computer, "I know that each person who hears your voice on the phone feels this is a friendly church." Leave one for the custodians on the restroom sink, "Thank you for serving without a spotlight."

Another option is to get the entire staff together and state in unhidden terms your positive feelings for each other. Pick out the best attribute of each staff person and share it with him or her.

6 **General Accountability.** "Confess your sins to each other and pray for each other so you may be healed" James 5:16. Accountability can be a bitter blessing. It's disturbing to bare ourselves to others, but when someone is there to challenge or convict us it helps us remain pure. If possible meet weekly to keep a general level of accountability. In a mixed group going deep may prove inappropriate, so you may decide to keep prayer, quiet time and character issues as fair culpability.

7 **Give In.** "No one takes my life from me," said Jesus, "I lay it down." Our Lord gave in for our benefit. He gave up His life for our salvation. Since He was willing to go to that length can't we give in some times? Every battle is not worth the blood. Every program is not worth tension. Every idea is not worth the anger.

Stubbornness acts a as curtain between two people. They each stand opposite of each other knowing the other is there but not able to see them. Giving in pulls back the curtain, revealing that the person is more important than a project.

8 **Become Friends.** Since you spend more time with your staff than anyone else on the planet, being friends would be a good move. Get to know each other. Ask about hobbies, books, and other things that they enjoy. Become a person your staff can depend on for support, love and care. Let then know that what goes for the teens goes for them when it comes to you being available for them no matter what time of the night or day.



9 **Fellowship.** Once a quarter meet at someone's home and eat together. Sharing a meal conveys friendship, acceptance, camaraderie, and the common goal of relishing a ton of calories. Choose a dessert like banana splits or some other make-it-yourself concoction. Then when you are unable to move break out the board games. What's the purpose? A staff that eats and plays together is able to work together more effectively.

10 **Biggest Fan.** Become each other's biggest fan. Never let a church member, or anyone else for that matter, hear you say anything negative about a staff member. Point out their great qualities. Take up for them when someone cuts him or her down.

An old acrostic for T.E.A.M. is Together Everyone Achieves More. The biggest fan concept makes T.E.A.M. a reality by putting all staff on the page. You may have personality differences, and may not agree on all ministry proposals, but it's hard to be against someone who brags about you and defends you.

TWENTY THREE

# 10 TECHNIQUES FOR PRAYER

**1 A.C.T.S.** Possibly the oldest and most used prayer technique out there. It doesn't go away because it is so useful and practical.

*Adoration.* Begin your prayer by praising God for who He is. Acknowledge Him as God the creator and establisher of all things.

*Confession.* When we confess He forgives. Be specific about the sin in your life. Sure, God already knows where we've been and what we've done; this allows us to hear it for ourselves.

*Thanksgiving.* Make a list of your blessings and then thank God for each one. Pour out your heart in appreciation of the gifts the Lord has freely given.

*Supplication.* Close with a period of requests. Pray for the lost, parents, teens or anything that you feel is critical to your ministry at this time.

**2 The Lord's Prayer.** The disciples didn't ask to learn how to do cool miracles. They didn't inquire about the inside track to raising the dead. They said, "Lord teach us to pray." Use the model Jesus gave in Luke 11:2-4. The twelve learned a prayer that honored God, affirmed His kingdom, trusted in His provision, depended on His forgiveness as others received their forgiveness, and relied on Him to deliver them from temptation.

**3 Life.** Some days are so rugged we need to spend time praying solely about life on this planet. Paul stated in Philippians 1:21b that dying is gain. Have you ever felt like that? If so, then pray for life. Pray that Christ would deliver the life He promised (John 10:10). Pray to feel the love that cannot be taken (Romans 8:31-39). Pray to live each day of your life for His glory (Colossians 3:17).

**4 Scripture.** A favorite prayer of mine is Habakkuk 3:2, "O Lord, we have heard of your fame, we stand in awe of your deeds, O Lord. Renew them in our day, in our time make them known." Utilize favorite passages as a way to connect with the pleas of various people who have expressed the same feelings to God. Pray with the psalmist, "As the deer pants for water, I thirst for You my God." Pray with John, "Even so, come Lord Jesus." Connect with God through His inspired Word.

**5 If...Then...** This is a dangerous prayer because you might receive what you are asking for. Read I Samuel 1, which contains the story of Hannah. She prayed, "Lord, if You will give me a child, then I will dedicate his life to Your service." What happened? Samuel, which means "asked of God," was born, and later Hannah took him to the temple to serve God. "If You will..." That's the easy part because it's God's part. "Then I'll..." That's the hard part because it is our part. It's a prayer vow, and if God delivers He expects you to do the same.



**6 Write It.** Get a few blank sheets of paper and write your thoughts to God. You'll catch yourself if you start to use redundant phrases, and you'll find yourself expressing yourself more clearly and passionately to the Lord.

**7 Positional Prayers.** 1) On your knees. Bow before the throne physically with your knees on the floor and head bent in reverence. 2) Prostrate. Spread out on the floor before the Almighty. 3) Stand with raised hands. Show the Father your empty hands and heart and tell Him that you want Him to fill them with His glory. You can decide on personal prayer positions, but they are powerful because they break us out of our normal prayer routines. In all other areas of life your posture reveals your heart. Do the same with God.

8. **Walking Prayers.** Walk through the neighborhood or community surrounding your building and pray for each family. You don't have to know their names, just pray that God will lead them to Christ through your church. Use a class period to get the youth group to take a 30 minute walk together and pray this way.

9. **Membership.** With a copy of your church membership directory in hand head off to a quiet spot. Pray over each name. Allow God's Spirit to bring to your heart what you should ask for each member. You may want to spend an extra amount of time praying for the parents of your teens and any struggles they may be experiencing.

10. **G.R.A.C.E.** This prayer is adapted from Heartlight.org.
*Glorify Your Name.* Ask God to receive all the credit.
*Renew My Passion.* Petition the Lord for a spiritual fire.
*Accept My Repentance.* Name specifically what you are turning from and who you are turning to.
*Care for the Broken.* Name the names of those who you know are hurting. Ask God to mend them.
*Empower Your Word.* Beg the Creator to make His words real in your life.

TWENTY FOUR

# 10 Tips for Staying in Tune with Teen Culture

1 **Watch from a Mall Bench.** The mall, can there be a better resource for diving into teen culture? Everywhere you look there are groups of teens. Groups of girls staring at the guys. Group of guys checking out the girls. All of them too embarrassed to approach each other. Notice the clothes they wear, the shops they enter, and the logos on the bags they carry. Each detail reveals what they feel is important. Taking note of such facets will give you the inside track to understand what makes them who and what they are.



2 **Listen to Their Music.** Unless you live in the same generation this could prove to be a painful experience. Each teen generation develops its own sound. The lyrics tend to represent their feelings. The 50's rang with innocence with a hair of dare. The 60's issued a tone of freedom laced with love. The 70's sang of self-reliance. The 80's of reckless abandon. The early 90's brought the grunge sound of depression. The late 90's delivered new teen idols with a popular pop beat. It's hard to tell if the music mimics the culture or vice versa, but either way it represents them well.

3 **Tune in to Their Favorite Television Programs.** Statistics show that the average teen watches between three and seven hours of television a day. My guess is that most of that time isn't spent on the Weather Channel. Televi-

sion helps produce their humor, their wardrobe, and their style.

Use TV as a tool to strengthen your teaching by playing some video clips of teens' favorite shows and getting into God's Word to decide if the situation displayed was helpful or harmful in following Christ. Make sure your church has the proper copyright license before showing videos.

4 **MTV.** A few months ago I was in Times Square in New York City. Gauging from the size and volume of the crowd outside of the Music Television studio it is safe to say that MTV is doing well at the moment. Regardless of how you personally feel about the broadcast company, you have to admit that they know their market. Several years ago it was popular to quote the CEO of MTV, who said, "We own fifteen year olds." Does that sounds like a strong assumption? Is it safe to say that MTV knows our teens better than we do? Learn from them and use their techniques to your advantage.

5 **Teen Magazines.** Teen, Seventeen, and others hold the pin-up stars of today. Bands, solo artists, and the cutest actors continue to be the wallpaper of many teens. These magazines let us know what teens view as attractive. They also tell us that many teens have a superficial view of themselves and others.



Use teen magazines as a teaching resource as well. Ask several students to bring some to class and divide into groups. Give each group a couple of magazines with the instruction to cut out the pictures of the prettiest and ugliest people in them. Show the photos to the class, then do a study of I Samuel 16:7.

6 **Latest Lingo.** Listen for the latest catch phrases, but take caution in using them. Teens might label you a geek, a nerd, or a dweeb (are those still used?) if you do. They won't think it's the bomb when you try to spit it out like them. Can they believe you're being for real when you act like such a lame loser by trying to talk like them? It's like, whatever.

7 **Movies.** Listen in shock as some of your group talks about the movies they watch. Sex scenes that get them fantasizing, language that would shame convicts, and violence that rivals any gang hit are the norm in today's flicks. Some view movies as nothing more than entertainment. The Lord said, "Be holy as I am holy." Can our teens watch in a spirit of holiness? Can we truly say that the film exalts God?

8 **Their Heroes.** Who do they wear on their tee-shirts? Whose name comes up in their conversations? Who is the most popular person in their life? Some teens adopt the style of their heroes. Others try to mimic their walk or talk. When Madonna first hit the scene thousands of teenage girls, and some guys, dressed like her. They wanted to become like their hero.

Employ mentoring in your group to provide positive role models for the teens. All the images they see from the world lead to a false sense of security. By placing a spiritually strong adult in their lives teens can see what a real hero is like.



9 **Fashion**. From dyed hair, to ragged jeans with enough chains hanging off for Harry Houdini to get nervous, teens make a statement with their clothing. Their style may reveal the type group they hang out with, or that they choose to be different. It may be a statement of rebellion or an attempt to fit in. Like music, every generation has its own look. Unless the image is ungodly don't worry too much. Just pray that baby blue polyester doesn't make a comeback.

10 **Quiz their Parents?** No offense, but most parents have little clue about what goes on in the life of their teen. Some parents view every style of song and clothing as an act of defiance. Have you ever heard a teen say, "My folks just don't understand me"? Parents are a great source for understanding the problems that result from some of the previous items in this list, but as far as giving keen insight into teen culture, sorry, no.

TWENTY FIVE

# 10 TIPS FOR PRESERVING YOUR INTEGRITY

1 **Love People.** "Love your neighbor as yourself" (Mark 12:31). Jesus said, "This is how all men will know you are my disciples, if you love each other" (John 13:35). Integrity is based on confidence and assurance. If someone feels that we don't love others, they begin to wonder what we are all about. They want to know why we are in ministry.



Displaying a heart that goes out to people in love builds their trust in your motives. A loving spirit makes friends of enemies and sees the best in each individual.

2 **Give God the Glory.** "Praise be to the God and Father of our Lord Jesus Christ, who has blessed us in the heavenly realms with every spiritual blessing in Christ" (Ephesians 1:3). When Paul wrote to the church in Ephesus, he didn't remind them of all the great things he did, but of what God did and does. Point to God when others point to you. Say something like, "You are very gracious, thank you." Be careful of over spiritualizing as one example gives: After a lesson the preacher stood by the door receiving accolades. When one man really expressed his thankfulness the preacher said, "It wasn't me, it was the Lord." The man replied, "Well, let's not get crazy. It wasn't that good."

3 **Help the Hurting Heal.** "Bear one another's burdens," (Galatians 6:2). The wounded surround us. Every heart has a hole. Every life contains a secret pain. Who doesn't ache from some battle? We all put on the mask and hide our feelings, so as ministers our responsibility lies in letting others know it's all right to show their scars. Redirect them to the Great Physician whose medicine treats all illnesses and heals all wounds.

4 **Develop Character.** "...also named Barnabas by the apostles (which is translated Son of Encouragement)..." Acts 4:36. Why did the apostles give Joses a name change to Barnabas? Because it described his character. Encouragement became a synonym for him. When people think of you what do they think of? If your name could be changed to represent your character what would be your new name? Acquire and keep integrity by forging moral values, spiritual absolutes, and virtues that cannot be bent under any circumstances.



5 **Give an Ear to Your Critics.** "Then the whole congregation of the children of Israel complained against Moses and Aaron in the wilderness" Exodus 16:2. Read that passage two more times if you've ever felt like the church hated you. Moses had it rough with that bunch of crybabies in the wild. Instead of ignoring them like most of us would do, instead of considering the source, instead of whining to Aaron about that poor assignment, Moses listened to the people on several occasions and implored God on their behalf. What did the people do in return besides weep more later? They followed him. More people will follow our lead when we listen than when we disregard.

6 **Admit Wrongs and Apologize.** "Have mercy on me, O God...blot out my sins...cleanse me from my sin" (Psalm 51:1-2). When we blow it let's admit it pronto and say we're sorry. Don't give people time to sit around talking about how things were mishandled, or wondering how long it will take before an apology arrives. There's nothing wrong with being wrong, just don't let it be for long.

7 **Present Second Chances.** "Get Mark and bring him with you for he is helpful for my ministry" (2 Timothy 4:11). You might remember that John Mark left Paul's mission trip in Acts 13:13. After that Paul and Barnabas argued about taking him on another trip and Paul refused. It appears that some time later Paul gave a second chance. We should do the same. After all, I remember being given a second chance, don't you?

8 **Be Authentic.** "Be careful not to give to a cause so others will see you and think a lot of you" (Matthew 6:1). Jesus used the term hypocrite to describe people who spoke one way and lived another. Our lives should be genuine and transparent. Suppose we live behind a mask all the time, what good does it do? We hide most of ourselves because we are afraid of people being disappointed if they discover the real us. The real disappointment enters when they learn we have lied with our life.

9 **Be Ethical.** "Ananias, why has Satan filled your heart to lie to the Holy Spirit and keep back part of the price of the land?" (Acts 5:3). Did you turn all remaining funds back in after the trip? Did you tell the truth, the whole truth, and nothing but the truth when it came to the details about the broken glass in the sanctuary?

10 **All Things.** "In all things showing yourself to be an example of good works; in doctrine showing integrity, reverence, incorruptibility, sound speech that cannot be condemned, that one who may be an opponent may be ashamed, having nothing evil to say about you" (Titus 2:7-8). That's the true challenge of integrity!

TWENTY SIX

# 10 Advantages of a Large Group

1 **More Students on a Mission.** Jesus said, The harvest is plentiful, but the laborers are few." Bigger groups have more people available for the harvest and can become more focused with their energy to bring in the crop.

Poll your group to determine just how many true harvesters you can count on. Form a school or community mission team determined to share Jesus with their friends and even those they don't know at this time.

2 **Greater Number of Leaders.** A mature larger group should yield a larger number of teens willing to serve in a leadership capacity. And because of the size of the crew you can expect a higher standard since there are so many willing to take a leadership position. There's no reason to settle for less than the best, so use a focused selection process as you install new youth leaders.

3 **Diversity.** Look over your roll. How many African Americans do you have? How many Caucasians? How many Asians? How many whiz kids? How many struggling teens? How many spiritually mature? How many.........

More young people can be reached because of the diversity of your group. We all tend to surround ourselves with people like us. Your group has the ability to envelop a host of teens for God. Bolster the group with the thought that their differences actually become a tool for the Lord to use for His purposes. Instead of viewing the teens as a melting pot of turmoil, view them as a heavenly mix of divine design.

4. **Larger Budget.** Of course the budget has the ability to be used faster, but still you have more resources than a smaller group. Even with all the inexpensive ways to promote and establish a great ministry, it's nice to know the funds are available when you need them.

Be specific with your budget process each year. When a youth ministry receives a good bit from the church some members become skeptical. Present a budget that will reveal ahead of time what the money will be going toward.

5. **Volunteer Base.** Can you ever have enough people willing to work in your ministry? We all have horror stories of vigilante volunteers set on breaking down and rebuilding the group, so be choosy with those who pitch in. With a large volunteer base you can afford to be more stringent and accept a higher motivated and centered worker. 10 X 50 includes ten questions to ask volunteers so you can make sure you're getting the best of the best.

6. **Abundance of Spiritual Gifts and Talents.** Let's separate a gift from a talent. A spiritual gift is a way to serve God that He gave you at rebirth into His kingdom. They are spirit-powered tools used solely for God's glory. A talent often is evident since physical birth. It may or may not be used for God glory. A singer may have vocal talent, but not a spiritual gift for evangelism if he or she is not a Christian.

Survey your group to determine each gift and talent represented in the group. Doing so will help you determine who needs to be on the leadership team and who needs to be part of the drama team. Don't use gifts and talents as a way of dividing the group, but as a way of using each individual's full potential for God's glory.

7 **High Energy Atmosphere.** The more people the greater the possibility for an electric atmosphere. Laughter, excitement, and intensity are all contagious. The more people you can pack into one place, the more it will multiply. Use small groups for intimate studies. Use large group gatherings for celebrations that can't be challenged by the world.

8 **Training Ground for Interns.** Smaller ministries often have a difficult time convincing the church leaders of the importance of interns. The larger ministry may be able to have multiple interns for guys and girls. The interns get to witness the dynamics of working with large and small groups. They'll learn the ins and outs of budgeting, planning, and getting prepared for retreats and such. Even if they don't begin full-time ministry at a large church, interns will find it easier to work with a smaller number having been with large numbers.

9 **Attracts the Unchurched.** To unbelievers a big group means something big time is happening. They find it hard to believe that so many people could be wrong. Plus they get to attend and blend in with the crowd. It's possible that no one will know they are a guest because no one in the group knows everyone else. As mentioned in #4 the larger budget will allow for grand events that the unchurched might find attractive.

10 **Contagious Praise and Worship.** Although private worship is wonderful it rarely has the emotion and power of a large group community setting. Seeing others let go and worship somehow makes you feel like everything will be alright. When your group is able to release their praise to God freely in mass meetings they will acquire the ability to take that same spirit and apply it to their daily walk.

TWENTY SEVEN

# 10 Wing-It Lessons

## 1 I Am Not Ashamed

1. I Am Not Ashamed of My Lifestyle (Philippians 1:19-21)
2. I Am Not Ashamed of Christ (II Timothy 7:7-8)
3. I Am Not Ashamed of the Gospel (Romans 1:16)

## 2 Let's Get Personal

1. Personal Faith (Romans 5:1-2)
2. Personal Savior (Romans 5:6-8)
3. Personal Relationship (Romans 5:9-11)

## 3 Evidence of Hanging Out with Jesus

1. Proof (Acts 3:1-10, 4:14-16)
2. Persecution (Acts 4:17-18)
3. Passion (Acts 4:19-20)
4. Praise (Acts 4:21-22)
5. Prayer (Acts 4:23-31

## 4 Growing Up in the Lord

Watch Jesus GROW with

**G**od (Luke 2:41-52)
**R**eputation (Mark 1:44-45, Matthew 9:31)
**O**thers (Luke 4:22)
**W**isdom (Matthew 13:53-54)

## 5 Worship

Worship is Intentional, Not Random
(II Samuel 6:1-2)
Worship is Fact Based, Not Feeling Driven
(II Samuel 6:3-8)
Worship is Life Changing, Not Lifeless
(II Samuel 6:9-13)
Worship is Participation, Not Performance
(II Samuel 6:14-19)
Worship is Relationship, Not Ritual
(II Samuel 6:20-22)

## 6 Real Value



Fellowship = Openness (I John 1:3-4)
Walking in the Light = Blamelessness (I John 1:5-9)
Hating the World = Holiness (I John 2:15-17)
Loving One Another = Togetherness (I John 4:7-8, 19-21)
Knowing = Blessedness (I John 5:13-15)

## 7 Jesus' Phrases are Our Prayers

Forgive Me (Luke 23:34
Care for Me (John 19:26)
Strengthen Me (John 19:28)
Save Me (Luke 23:43)
Be with Me (Matthew 27:46)
Hold Me (Luke 23:46)
Crown Me (John 19:30)

## 8 Like a Child Become... (Matthew 18:1-6, 10-14)

**C**hanged
**H**umble
**I**nnocent
**L**ittle
**D**ependent

## 9 God Loves You

God the Father Loves You! He Sent His Son
(John 3:16)
God the Son Loves You! He Died for You
(I Corinthians 15:1-4)
God the Holy Spirit Loves You! He Lives within You
(Romans 8:5-11)

## 10 We're Free!

Free to Hear the Voice of God (John 10:27)
Free to Talk to God (Matthew 21:22)
Free to Express God (2 Samuel 6:21)
Free to Experience God (Joshua 24:31)
Free to Follow God (Matthew 4:19)

These lessons are not here to give you an excuse to wing-it. Break open these pages only in case of emergency.

## TWENTY EIGHT

# 10 Tips for Long Haul Youth Ministry

1 **Continually Reestablish Your Commitment.** Each year thousands of married couples renew their vows. They do this to remind each other of the promises instituted on their wedding day. Unlike those couples, those of us in ministry gravitate toward replaying the same life year after year until we start wondering what we are doing in ministry.

Sit down and write out a ministry statement. Record what first drew you to ministry. What driving force consumed you in the early years of the work? Journal your hopes and dreams for all teens. After you have done this put it in your daily notes or in a file that you frequent. At least once every two months get the statement out to refresh those vows and purposes for the ministry. Pull them out even more during the draining times.

2 **See the Future in the Present.** Paul wrote that he pressed "toward the goal for the prize of the upward call of God" (Philippians 3:14). He found sustaining strength by seeing and pressing toward the goal, the end result in Christ.

Youth ministry often resembles farming; you plant a seed in one season and reap in another. You may plant the Word in the heart of a young person and not see fruit until their mid 20's or 30's. Because of our desire to see instantaneous results, we get discouraged when things don't fall into place. But by seeing the fruit, the future, while we are planting in the present we can find sustaining strength for the long haul.

3 **Be Dedicated to Youth Ministry.** Some youth workers view student ministry as a stepping stone to preaching full time. They see it as the normal route to take because they are "too young" or "inexperienced" to lead a church.

Create a vision in your heart for teens. Realize that no one would like to have a new set of parents every year and a half, so determine to stay put and in youth work until you know God wants a change.

4 **Evaluate and Grow.** Whether through activities, messages, or personal walk, learn to evaluate and expand your ministry. After any of those you may want to take thirty minutes or an hour and jot down what went right, what went wrong, and how to improve. There's no need to over analyze or beat yourself up, just be logical and see things through the clearest lens possible.



5 **Get ESP.** In my ministry we encourage everyone to have ESP - Emotional, Spiritual, and Physical health. You need ESP for a balanced life no matter who you are, but especially in ministry. Emotional health is for the counseling, calls, and mental toughness required to work with some of the membership. Spiritual health calls for a daily walk with God because people expect you to know Him if you are leading them to know Him. And Physical health permits lock-ins, pizza parties, and an irregular schedule that comes with the territory. When others ask you how you have lasted so long in youth ministry just tell them you have ESP.

6 **Resolve to Communicate Successfully.** Focus your communication skills in two areas: Mass and micro. See mass communication as the proficiency to inform large groups of people in a way they will understand. Let your

mail outs and phone messages be to the point.

Think about micro-communication as being your classes and talks. Strive to be the best teacher you can be. Learn to communicate to teens in a relevant and interesting fashion. Because each generation is different you can't keep one style for your career.

7 **Minister to the Entire Family.** For years youth work held the reputation of being a babysitting service for teens. Youth ministers were referred to as youth directors and were not taken seriously. To remain hearty in youth work, focus on the family, not just the teens. Provide a comprehensive ministry that reaches out to each family member and places each of you on the same team.

8 **Share Your Responsibilities.** Recently, I learned a true secret to long term youth ministry. A friend said, "Don't do it all." That doesn't sound like much of a secret, right? Then why aren't more youth ministers doing it? Most of us try to do everything ourselves. That's a great formula for burnout. Do what you must do, then use teens, parents, and volunteers to do the rest as you supervise and train them.



9 **Become a Student of Parents and Youth.** Away from the ministry hang out with some of the families in your group and observe them. Take note of how they relate to each other. Use these mental notes to compare with other families and soon you will discover why some families click and others don't. Of course each family is different so don't use these as stereotypes, but as tools to keep you in tune.

10 **Don't Neglect Your Family.** Though last on this list it is your first priority. A married couple needs to have time alone away from the ministry. A single may need to take the holidays and fly home to visit with family members. As you work with the families of others, keep your family tight and you will always have someone to turn to during the long haul of ministry.

Twenty Nine

# 10 Tips for Selecting A Retreat Facility

1 **Settle on a Purpose.** Your purpose will decide what type of facility will work best. A youth group wanting a fun weekend together may put a high priority on recreational facilities. Perhaps you want to work in some sightseeing into the weekend, then you might want to select an area that is close to the attractions you would like to visit.



2 **Length of Stay.** Consider the advantages of a second night at a facility to provide more time for group interaction. Veteran retreat planners have discovered that the second night goes a long way in creating a valuable community experience. Factor in travel time as well. You may be planning a three day retreat, but if it takes a day to get there then you really have only one day to work with.

3 **Reserve Early.** The best dates and nicest facilities get booked first. Consider reserving a facility six months to a year before you want to have a retreat. If you are pleased with the facility and service, you might want to make your reservation for the following year before your retreat is over.

4 **Decide on a Price Range.** It is wise to go with what the majority of your group is willing to spend. Consider offering financial assistance to those needing help. Or you can charge your group a little less than the actual cost

and ask several people who can afford it to help make up the difference.

5 **Get Organized.** Before you call a facility, do your planning. Decide what type of accommodations you want (motel, dorms or cabins), what type of meal service, quality of menu--tuna surprise or Chicken Kiev; how large your group will be, what kind of meeting space you'll need, when you plan to arrive and depart, and if you mind sharing a facility with other groups.

6 **Have a "Plan B".** Have several options on dates that would work for your group. Locking yourself in to a specific date without options will set you up for disappointment if the center is not available at that particular time. Confirm dates for a facility before you confirm dates with a speaker!

7 **Compare.** When comparing prices between retreat facilities, make sure you ask what is and is not included in the basic fee, such as coffee breaks, audio/visual equipment and recreational equipment. Talk to other groups and find out where they have received the best service. Make a visit to a potential site. Talking in person with a representative at the facility and seeing the buildings and grounds will answer a lot of questions. When you compare facilities, don't let cost be the primary factor--ask yourself which facility and staff will help your group best achieve its retreat program goals.

8 **Get it in Writing.** You will want to have a written contract signed by your group representative and by the retreat facility's representative describing the agreement between the group and the conference center [camp]. Usually a nonrefundable deposit (10-15% of the minimum fee) will be required. Be sure that the minimum number of participants and the corresponding minimum fee are reasonably attainable. You may be required to make up the difference if you miss your minimum. Ask if there are additional cancellation charges.

9 **Evaluate.** Check out the staff's attitude toward service and hospitality as well as their philosophy. Ask others who have been there. Will a host be available to answer your questions and take care of needs during the retreat?

10 **Do Your Homework.** Know what you and your group want and ask lots of questions. Pre-retreat communication pays off. Keep notes and names of those you talked with for all your phone conversations, and make sure all agreements and arrangements are made in writing. Frequent and detailed pre-retreat communication will improve your chances of getting the level of service that is so important in making your retreat experience a positive one.

**Need help finding a retreat site?**
Check the ELCA Outdoor Ministries Directory or call the ELCA Outdoor Ministries staff at 1-800/638-3522, extension 2593.

THIRTY

# 10 Techniques for Recognizing Suicidal Teens

Nobody will even notice I'm gone.

1 **Previous Attempts.** When a teen develops a pattern of suicide attempts the following items in this category become even more significant and necessary to watch. Teens with a record of trying to take their lives lean toward repeating the attempt again and again. Although some feel that this is a cry for attention or love it cannot be ignored because an attempt may lead to success.



Tip: Seek professional assistance. Though that's common sense, it's possible for some parents to reject the idea because of pride or believing it's a phase of life.

2 **Drug and Alcohol Abuse.** Teens who show signs of depression in addition to links with drugs and alcohol consumption are a risk for suicide. Their feelings of inadequacy coupled with the availability of controlled substances present opportunity. They can consider pills or potions as a painless way to end their lives.

3 **Rejection.** Adolescents who wrap their entire lives around certain events or people consider suicide when expectations and reality collide. They might feel rejected by a parent for never making the grade. They may feel discarded by a close friend. Perhaps they were told the starting position on the team was guaranteed and they

didn't make third string.

**4** **Self-Destructive Behavior.** Reckless driving, advanced risk taking, and "cheating death" all are typical signs of those who are suicidal. They lack a respect for life, therefore they tempt death because they feel that either way they win.

**5** **Sudden Changes in Mood and Media Influences.** Suicidal urges often represent themselves in rapid mood swings, defensive behavior, and viewing and listening to media that glorifies death. After exhibiting this type of behavior, a teen may suddenly become at peace and act as if all negatives have been resolved. Sometimes the thought of the finality of suicide brings a peace and calm to the individual about to make an attempt.

A person who is contemplating taking his or her own life may show one or more signs. However, Christine M. Sadowski, Ph. D., a child and family psychologist at Mayo Clinic, notes "...it's important to keep in mind that the warning signs are only guidelines." There is no one type of suicidal person. If you are concerned that someone is contemplating suicide — for whatever reason — arrange professional assistance for that person immediately.—Mayo Clinic Report



**6** **Unexpected Crisis or Trauma.** Surprise disruptions of life can trigger suicidal thoughts by rapidly placing a teen in unfamiliar emotional territory. The loss of a parent through death or divorce, moving to a new community and being rejected, the suicide of a close friend, and other distressing events frequently influence those who take their lives.

**7** **Communicating About Death.** When a teen writes poetry or songs, or talks about suicide in more than an inquisitive fashion, take this as a cry for help. Most individuals thinking about suicide use a variety of means to let you discover their plans without saying it directly.

**8** **Giving Away Possessions.** It's one thing to give away old clothes to a charity, it's another to give your best friend your favorite jewelry or other prized belongings. "I'm not going to need this anymore," has been heard by thousands of friends before a life was taken.

9 **Withdrawal.** Suicidal teens often retreat from their friends, clubs, team, family, and the church. They shut themselves off from the world in order to convince themselves that they are not important to those around them. Their grades suffer, they shirk their responsibilities, and disregard their promises.

10 **Guilt.** Guilt from sin, guilt from embarrassment, guilt from bringing shame on the family can induce suicide. A teen arrested for driving under the influence may take their life because they don't feel they could ever be forgiven, or because they feel they embarrassed their family.

For facts on suicide and for more prevention tips logon to:

http://www.cdc.gov/ncipc/dvp/suifacts.htm

Center for Disease Control and Prevention

## THIRTY ONE

# 10 Tips for Building a Committed Team

1 **Define and Communicate Responsibilities that Challenge.** Communicate the big picture and how people fit into it. It is much easier to put a jigsaw puzzle together if you can see the completed picture on the puzzle box. It is important for people to have a clear picture of the goals and objectives and how they fit into the plan.

Next, communicate specific responsibilities to the team members. What do you expect from them? Provide a clear ministry description and allow their input. A good ministry description states specific responsibilities, how much authority the team members have, and to whom they are accountable, what benefits they have, and the length of time they are to serve. Help them take ownership of the goals, tasks, and responsibilities. Encourage their input and provide the opportunity for them to set their own goals as part of the total plan

2 **Give Authority Equal to the Responsibility.** One of the most frequent complaints of team members is that they are given responsibility without corresponding authority. Leaders need to be willing to trust those they ask to do a job by giving them the authority necessary to do the job. How much authority should be given? Enough to get the job done. This authority should be communicated to those with whom the leaders work.

Increase authority when performance earns it and responsibility requires it. As people increase in skills and effectiveness, increase their authority. This will raise morale and increase the effectiveness of the team.

**3 Establish Standards for Excellence.** Every team should have a set of realistic operating standards. Some specific standards that will increase team effectiveness might include these: "We honor our commitments. We believe in being people of character and integrity. We are faithful to our responsibilities. We are wise stewards of our time, talents, and resources. We work together as a team. We agree to disagree, but not disagreeably. We are committed to ongoing training and development. We are committed to excellence. We are committed to results, not just performance." As a leader, you must set the example. The standards will become team standards only when they see you maintaining them.

**4 Train Leaders in the Skills Necessary to Meet the Standards.** Make training and mentoring a priority. Training is the key to an effective team. No team wins without training and practice. A good leader never does the job alone. Churches that are in decline have leaders who see their jobs as doing the ministry for the people and vice versa. However, in growing churches, leaders equip and mobilize people for the work of ministry.

**5 Provide the Knowledge and Information People Need to Succeed.** They need information about organizational goals, plans, and changes. Workers are motivated when they know what is happening in the organization. It makes them feel important and valuable, helps them desire to do a better job, and enables them to do a better job. Without information, people cannot take responsibility, will not be as creative, and will not be as productive.

**6 Provide Appropriate, Positive Feedback.** Regularly reinforce positive performance. Compliments, cards, notes, rewards, and advancement are some ways to reinforce excellent performance. Feedback should be tailored to the person, performance, and situation. Morale and effectiveness increase when people receive regular feedback.

**7 Recognize and Reward Efforts and Achievements.** You get what you reward. Make heroes of your people. Public recognition and rewards are essential. Shine the spotlight on accomplishments. Pictures, awards, speeches, plaques, and newsletters are just a few ways to recognize accomplishments. Everyone has an invisible sign hung around his neck that says, PMMFI (pum-fee) -- Please Make Me Feel Important. Recognition does that and builds a better team.

**8 Trust Your Team.** Ralph Waldo Emerson said, "Trust men, and they will be true to you; treat them greatly, and they will show themselves great." Building trusting relationships is essential. A leader can demonstrate trust in many ways: Be sensitive to needs, interests, and concerns. Listen to ideas, dreams, and plans. Delegate, or trust, with significant assignments or responsibilities.

Distinguish between trust in character and trust in ability. Some have strong, mature character but little ability. Others have less mature character but great ability. Trusting people at the highest degree possible helps them develop a higher level of both character and ability.

**9 Give Permission to Fail.** View failure as a growing experience. The only failure is one we don't learn from. Establish some guidelines for failure: It is OK to make a mistake. It is OK to fail if we are doing our best. When we fail, we can talk about what went wrong, what we can learn, and how to do better.

**10 Treat Others with Respect.** Treating team members with respect increases motivation. People work best when they feel valued and respected. Demonstrate your commitment and loyalty the same way you expect others to be committed and loyal to you as the leader.

## THIRTY TWO

# 10 Natural Techniques for Teen Faith Sharing

1 **Faithful Example.** In *Experiencing God*, Henry Blackaby wrote, "What you do reveals what you believe about God regardless of what you say." When teens live Christ their faith will be shared with others without their having to be brass or loud about it. The goal is to produce a consistent lifestyle through the power of the Spirit. Galatians 5:21-22 speaks about the fruit that the Spirit yields. When love, joy, peace, patience, kindness, goodness, faithfulness, gentleness and self-control flow out of a teen's life, Christ can't help but get noticed.

2 **A Personal Testimony.** People take the stand in a court room to tell an account of what they witnessed. A personal testimony develops when a young person witnesses changes in their lives through a relationship with Christ. It allows a teen to say, "I used to be like this.... but because of Christ this has happened...."

Some long time believing teens get discouraged because they feel they don't have a life altering testimony. They think a radical turn around is the only thing that speaks to others. Let them know that the change is what is important and that God can use them to help others who don't feel like they are all that bad to see the goodness of Christ.

3 **Invitations to Events.** Andrew invited Peter to meet Jesus. Philip invited Nathaniel to meet the Lord. The

woman at the well invited her entire town to "come and see the one who told me everything I ever did." A causal invitation can be used by God to increase His kingdom.

Keep the group informed of every event and activity so they can be prepared to invite their friends. Dates, times, what to bring, and other information should all be clear so the invitation can be clear as well.

4 **T-shirts.** Christian apparel continues to remain popular among the saved. The unsaved notice it as well and take it as a reflection of your beliefs. As mentioned earlier in the book be sure to wear non-offensive clothing. Slogans about hell, abortion, homosexuality, and other inciting issues hold the power to do more harm than good. The message may be right on target, but the spirit in which it is received may cause a person to run from, rather than to Christ.

5 **Help Others with Problems.** Being a friend, listening, and offering advice go a long way in acting as the light of the world. When teens find that their Christian friends are willing to offer more than lip service to their problems their curiosity is piqued. They want to know why a person would help another without expecting anything in return. This is a huge opportunity for teens to share their faith because what day goes by that the average teen doesn't have a problem?



6 **Study One on One.** Some in your group may find they have the gift of evangelism. While some teens wear t-shirts and others are making invitations this group is busy setting up the next study. (Isn't it great how God can use each person differently?)

For teens with this gift, be sure to encourage them to take advantage of the time before and after school, and lunch as critical times for their outreach. You may want to buy them a daily planner so they can schedule the studies they have.

7 **Hang Time.** Unscheduled time holds valuable moments for God. On the bus on the way to a game; in the hall

between classes; at the mall on a Saturday; waiting in line for a movie ticket. Explain to teens that each minute holds the possibility to share Jesus with another. As they hang out with their friends tell them to look for opportunities to talk about their faith.

8 **A Phone Call a Day.** A note would work well too. Challenge your group to make one call, or write one note a day to someone they know who isn't a Christian. The call can last ten seconds and be used to invite someone to something, ask about homework, or anything else. Jesus doesn't have to be specifically mentioned. The call or note will let the other person know that someone is thinking about him in a caring way.

9 **Relationships Through Service.** Get teens to get involved in community service outside the church. They will meet new friends and create a chance to tell about the Servant King. Service makes us get out of the way and put others first. It opens us up not only to give, but to receive a blessing from that service. Perhaps the blessing some receive will be Jesus.



10 **Encouragement.** Encourage teens to encourage. A positive young person will get to share their faith a lot more than a negative one.. A discouraging person repels people, while an encouraging person draws them near.

THIRTY THREE

# 10 ?'s to Ask an Interviewing Intern

**1 How Would You Describe Your Relationship with God?** Listen for terms of intimacy and devotion. If the intern is young you don't need to expect the maturity that develops with years of time with the Lord; however, there should be evidence of a personal faith.

Take it deeper by asking the potential intern to write about his or her relationship. Many people find that they can express their feelings better on a page than out loud. Tell them to be honest and not to write what they think you want to hear.

**2 How Is A Person Born Again?** Make sure they provide Scripture references with their answer. An intern may be no Bible scholar, but they need to know the gospel by book, chapter and verse. Part of the role in developing a youth group is being able to teach teens how to lead a friend to Jesus. They also need to have the salvation plan for man memorized for times when they have occasion to share it with students with whom they come in contact.

**3 What Do You Expect to Gain from this Internship?** The answer to this question will determine two things. First, it will render a clear mental picture of the intern. We have all discovered that we become what we envision. The child that was called dumb in the early years grows up believing he is dumb because of the picture presented. When a positive picture is shared it often it proves itself true in life.

Second, it will give the intern value and measurement. Halfway through the internship she or he may perceive that they are nowhere near their original goal for joining the ministry. They can then adjust the direction to pull back in line with the desired result.

4 **How Did You Come to Christ?** In essence no one's story is any more or less than another's. The purpose of the question is to allow the one interviewed to share their life. We say that commitment to Christ is the most important decision in a person's life. Since this is true permit a detailed recount of the events that brought about the transformation.

5 **What Led You to Youth Ministry?** This is their chance to share their heart for teenagers. I firmly believe you need to have a special spirit for youth or it will be like walking into a minefield wearing a blindfold. Teens can be the most loving, or the most hateful. They can brag on you one minute and cut you down the next.

"Uuuuummmm, I thought it was as good a ministry as any" isn't going to get it. Ask them to tell you and your team specifically why they feel they must work with youth over all the other ministry areas in the church.

6 **Do You Have Any Prior Arrests?** I know this sounds like a question off a form you fill out at the employment office, but it is necessary. Sex offenders and other criminals seek churches out as places of employment to gratify their longings. Trusting a smile and sweet words will be a poor excuse if something happens to the youth. You will need to run a background check on all people about to receive employment. It doesn't mean you don't trust him or her, it means that you are being wise. I've noticed that people with convictions in the past that feel they have obtained forgiveness and made restitution tend not to hide the past. Those who feel it is still a

problem are more likely to hide it.

> TAKE YOUR TIME WITH THE INTERVIEW PROCESS AND DO NOT SETTLE FOR LESS THAN THE BEST. IF AN INTERN IS GOING TO BE WITH YOU FOR A YEAR OR MORE YOU CANNOT AFFORD A MISTAKE IN SELECTION.

7 **How Will You Handle...?** Unravel a list of possible circumstances. How will you handle an emergency if you have an accident? What will you do if you find a guy and girl in bed together at the retreat? The group vandalizes a hotel room, what will you do? Be as specific as you can so the scenarios are clear.

8 **What Is Your Spiritual Gift?** Awareness of their spiritual gift will show that an intern is in touch with his or her spiritual influence. They will know how they can best reach teens through the use of the gift. Ask him or her to share a time when God worked through His gift. Allow them to tell how it has impacted the lives of others. This isn't a time to shine the light on them, but on God. Listen for terms of self glory or God's glory.



9 **What Is Your Greatest Weakness?** In the above question they got to depict a strength. Now they get to talk about the ways they are not so strong. This will help you determine if you are interviewing a person who is conscious of their weaknesses, or a person who is insecure. An insecure person is going to need constant pats and attention for them to feel worthy. A person who knows their weakness, but doesn't allow it to burden them can be used by God despite the weakness.

10 **What Do You Believe Is God's Vision for Teens?** Listen for passion and love. The question is not easy and should be answered deeper than, "For all teens to come to know Jesus." Provide them the opportunity to share long term vision and plans for youth ministry.

THIRTY FOUR

# 10 Techniques to Stretch Your Sense of Humor

1 **Read the Comics.** If for no other reason subscribe to a paper for the comic section. World crisis? Who cares. Garfield? Now we're getting down to business. The absolute best comic strip for youth ministers is Zits. Jeremy, the teenage character in the comic, represents teens to perfection.

2 **Rent and *Watch Bill Cosby Himself.*** Warning: the last few minutes of the video contains inappropriate material. Other than that it is hilarious. It's the kind of video you can watch time and time again and laugh just as hard. Bill Cosby has a talent for taking average family situations and bringing out the humor.

3 **Exaggerate the Moment.** Most humor comes from sources that involved intense emotions. When was the last time you were extremely mad or sad? Take those feelings and exaggerate them and it's a recipe for humor. We need to be able to laugh at the things that got us so mad. In most cases there's no real reason to be upset, so why not laugh about it?

4 **Buy a Joke Book.** This suggestion might be a joke because it's difficult to find a joke book with a lot of funny material in it—but if you enjoy knock, knock jokes then buy a book of them. If you like one liners then get the book.

Shop in a Christian store for your jokes or you're in for a shocking day. Unless you know exactly what you are looking for, stay away from the shelves of most bookstores. They carry enough filthy language and unfit humor to leave you scarred for life. The only reason to walk down that aisle is to pull your teens out of the store when you're at the mall with them.

5 **Make Faces.** Have you ever been driving down the road and a kid in the car next to you makes a face, or picks his nose at you? Are you the type person who tries to ignore the child only for him to turn up the charm and use two fingers in his nose? Don't just sit there, fight back! At the next traffic light press your face against your car window as hard as you can, cross your eyes, and blow air out of your mouth with as much force as possible. Within that instant the kid in the next vehicle will consider you the coolest or weirdest adult ever encountered. The boy's parent, however, will just think you strange (because they have no sense of humor and need to read this chapter).

Of course this technique isn't limited to the freeway. Practice faces at home in the mirror if they don't come naturally. Making faces proves to others that you are willing to break the barrier of normality and take a risk.



6 **See with a Smile.** Look for humor. Earlier we recommended learning about teen culture by sitting on a mall bench. That's a wonderful place to watch for humor. Be on the lookout for fighting couples. You don't need to hear their words; their actions speak louder. He'll be pleading and she'll be jerking away, swinging her purse in the process. Watch for the parent who is having to drag their child from the toy store as the tike points to the specific toy and screams. None of these instances are funny to the people they are happening to, so why is it alright to laugh? Because most of those same people will tell the story humorously to a friend within the week. You get the blessing of laughing earlier.

7 **Listen for Fun.** Go to a park and find a nice spot near a large group of people. Close your eyes and listen. Listen

for the laughter of children playing. Listen for adults cutting up in a loose minute. Listen for people blowing their car horns on the street. Listen for the footsteps of joggers. Let various sounds bring a smile through your ears. Enjoy the way the Father has created the possibility of joy in each activity.

8 **Weigh the Moment.** I'm not sure of the exact scientific figure, but I think it's safe to say that most folks are way too serious. To make sure you don't fit in that category think about how you weigh moments. Do you punish the teen who was five minutes late the same as the one who hot wired the bus and took a little drive? Overreacting to small infringements is a classic sign of taking life too seriously. What about other moments? What significance do you place on them? Take a some time and write down what really gets you angry.

1.

2.

3.

Are the things on the list worth it? Are they justified?

9 **Return to Childhood.** Another way adults can learn humor from children is to play. It's said that we play at our work and work at our play. We all need time to return to childhood and just have a good time. If you can find a deserted playground one afternoon take a few spins on the merry-go-round. Or swing high to the sky. Or coast down the slide. If you need an excuse then take a child with you and "pretend" to be playing with him. Then if other adults are present they won't think you're having a blast.

10 **I'm Funny.** Learn to laugh at yourself. When someone else makes fun of you, laugh and tell one on yourself that's even better. Laughing at yourself says that you are secure in who you are and you know how to weigh the moment.

## Thirty Five

# 10 Tips to Separate Good Ideas from God Ideas

1

**Good Ideas Often Bring Glory to Me.** When ideas are clever and seem above our standard level, people tend to oooh and ahh over the idea. They begin to tell others how lucky the church is to have us.

**God Ideas Always Point Back to Him.** After the parting of the Red Sea do you think anyone said, "Hey, Moses, that was so cool! Do it again!" God's children knew who did the miracle.

2

**Good Ideas Develop Out of My Will.** How do I want the ministry to grow? What program can I start to make sure the teens become what they should? How can I get the retreat center at the bottom of the slopes so we can ski in for lunch?

**God Ideas Always Conform to His Will.** It was God's idea to blow the walls of Jericho down from the inside out. Man wouldn't have come up with that plan. The marching and shouting idea came straight from God because it was the way He wanted it done. The Israelites would have designed another plan.

**Good Ideas Come About On My Schedule.** When something is our idea we can implement it at just about any time we choose. As long as it doesn't conflict with another event we can put it into action.

3

**God Ideas Take Place On God's Timing.** "You see, at just the right time, when we were still powerless, Christ died for the ungodly" Romans 5:6. God knows what the best time is for His ideas.

**Good Ideas Come from Dreams.** Dreams are not bad they just may not be God's. They are often fine goals that would be nice, but not necessarily necessary.

4

**God Ideas Come from a God-sized Vision.** When it's from God it's something that only God can do. Without His involvement it can't happen.

**Good Ideas are Optional.** If our ideas become reality that's wonderful, but if they don't nothing of eternal significance is lost. It would be nice if it did happen, but only disappointing if they don't.

5

**God Ideas are Mandatory.** If we fail to carryout a God idea then we are being disobedient. What if the apostles said, "Nice suggestion, but we'll try something else" after the Lord gave the great commission?

**Good Ideas Are Limited by Our Ability.** We are all talented in one or two areas, but beyond that we need help. With a good idea we plan and develop around our strengths. We avoid doing anything that will involve our weaknesses.

6

**God Ideas Are Not Limited.** Since nothing is impossible for God anything can happen. He already stated boldly that He can do "more than we can ask or imagine" (Ephesians 3:20). I've got a great imagination, so it's awesome knowing that He can do what I could never think up.

7

**Good Ideas Do a Lot of Talking.** Good ideas make sense and sound good. In fact, they are so believable that people are willing to sign up before there is any real proof that the idea will become a reality.

**God Ideas Do a Lot of Walking.** Regardless of whether people believe the God idea or not, there will be proof. Noah talked about the coming flood, but spoke with hammer and nails in hand. The ark gave merit to his message.

8

**Good Ideas Miscalculate the Bottom Line.** Most ideas fail along the way because the road gets too rough. People stumble under the load.

**God Ideas Count the Cost.** Everyone who God talked to knew there was a cost involved. Just ask Abraham as he and Isaac headed up the hill.

9

**Good Ideas are Fueled by Momentary Passion.** Like a salesman with a two minute offer many people jump on board with star glazed eyes and hearts on fire.

**God Ideas are Fueled by Faith.** After the passion fades, faith remains for those who are following a God idea. That's what kept Jesus moving toward the cross.

10

**Good Ideas are Man Led.** When people are following us it's a good idea. They may have great reasons for taking up the cause. We may be charismatic or have admirable qualities.

**God Ideas are Spirit Led.** In spite of an abundance of leadership skill, or the absence of any skill, when the people are following God and not us, it doesn't matter.

THIRTY SIX

# 10 Techniques to Develop Patience

1 **Get a Clear Picture of Yourself.** "The end of a matter is better than its beginning, and patience is better than pride" (Ecclesiates 7:8). One of the reasons we get so impatient is our pride. We mistakenly believe that everything depends on us. Our self importance sends us scurrying about in a frantic pace to complete all the things that only we can do. Develop patience by realizing that we don't have to do everything. With pride out of the way we can delegate to others and learn to relax.



2 **Let the Fruit Grow.** "But the fruit of the Spirit is love, joy, peace, patience..." (Galatians 5:22). An aspect of the Spirit's produce is patience. If we are allowing Him to have control of our lives then composure will be an unforced response. Our flesh causes us to get uptight. Our worldly thinking blossoms impatience. Paul wrote in Ephesians 5:18 that we are to get filled with the Spirit. He means that every area of our lives is to be intoxicated with His power.

3 **One Thing Leads to Another.** "And we pray this in order that you may live a life worthy of the Lord and may please him in every way: bearing fruit in every good work, growing in the knowledge of God, being strengthened with all power according to his glorious might so that you may have great endurance and patience, and

joyfully giving thanks to the Father, who has qualified you to share in the inheritance of the saints in the kingdom of light" (Colossians 1:10-12). Patience grows in our lives when we live according to God's will, do good, increase our knowledge of Him, and depend on His power for strength. Take each of those items out of our life and it's no wonder we feel perturbed.

4. **Put it On.** "Therefore, as God's chosen people, holy and dearly loved, clothe yourselves with compassion, kindness, humility, gentleness and patience" (Colossians 3:12). What did you wear today? What shirt did you choose? Chances are that you personally picked out your wardrobe. It was your choice. God tells us that patience is a choice as well. We can choose to put it on as part of our spiritual clothing, or leave it off and allow our fretfulness to remain exposed.

5. **Jesus' Perspective.** "But for that very reason I was shown mercy so that in me, the worst of sinners, Christ Jesus might display his unlimited patience as an example for those who would believe on him and receive eternal life" (I Timothy 1:16). Paul believed that his acceptance into the kingdom provided an example of God's unlimited patience. Since the Lord had such patience waiting on us to come to Him, we need to have the same patience when dealing with others. Paul wrote in Philippians 2:4, "Each of you should look not only to your own interests, but also to the interests of others."



6. **Pray About Everything.** "Worry about nothing, pray about everything" (Philippians 4:6). Everything? Yep. In other words, "Pray without ceasing" (I Thessalonians 5:17). In our haste to do everything ourselves we either forget to pray or don't feel like it is important enough. But God said pray about everything. There is no other way to interpret that except to do what He says. And in doing so we will find contentment and peace.

7. **Picture Noah.** "Preach the Word; be prepared in season and out of season; correct, rebuke and encourage--with great patience and careful instruction" (II Timothy 4:2).

Noah preached for 120 years without a single response. That's patience. We never see him questioning God. We never see him asking for a miracle to speed up the building process.

As we try to show Jesus to others discouragement can seep in when responses are few or nonexistent. In those times we need to remember our ark building friend who continued in God's will despite the lack of interest of his neighbors.

8 **Don't Get Lazy.** "We do not want you to become lazy, but to imitate those who through faith and patience inherit what has been promised" (Hebrews 6:12). Sometimes we try to get patience by procrastinating or erasing our to do list. Instead of working diligently toward the goal, we eliminate the goal and sit back. The Father warns us that laziness does not equal patience. In the place of laziness we need to draw on the experience of those who have packed schedules, yet refused to get burdened.



9 **Prophet Patience.** "Brothers, as an example of patience in the face of suffering, take the prophets who spoke in the name of the Lord" (James 5:10). Read the Old Testament prophets and you'll learn about having a bad day. God lets us know that seeing how they handled the pressures of life will give us insight and hope.

10 **Care Casting.** "Cast all your anxiety on him because he cares for you" (I Peter 5:17). A lack of patience can be summed up as a lack of trust in God. We try to handle everything because we don't believe He will come through for us. Peter makes it clear, we need to cast, to throw, everything His way because of His love for us.

THIRTY SEVEN

# 10 Cool Attributes of Jesus

**1 Jesus Turned Water into Wine...He's the Life of the Party** (John 2:1-11). How dare you think I just said that Jesus wants us to get drunk. Our culture depicts our Lord as a dull square who doesn't believe in fun. Present a picture of Christ that proves He not only knows how to have a good time, but that times are made better by His friendship.



**2 Jesus Fed 5,000...He's the Bread of Life** (Matthew 14:13-21). The always compassionate apostles were more than willing to send the crowd away with empty bellies, but not God. Jesus wanted the people to have a stomach that matched their brains after His lesson – filled! The miracle teaches us that our Lord cares about our bodies and spirits. He knows that it is difficult for us to follow spiritually when our hearts are carried away with thoughts of daily provisions.

**3 Jesus Kicks Out the Money Changers...He's the Defender of Righteousness** (Mark 11:15-19). If they had T-shirts back in the day of Christ, He could have worn one that said, "My Dad's Better Than Your Dad." Jesus was proud of His Father and He didn't like men making an unfair profit at the temple. For anyone who thought Jesus was soft or wimpy the picture of this passage shows that He was anything but a sissy. Why didn't the money changers fight back? Why didn't they turn Him over to the authorities? The only reason that comes to mind is that they didn't think they could take Him in a fair fight. And the only reason for that is because He was a real man.

4 **Jesus Stills a Storm...He Can Catch a Wave** (Luke 8:22-25). We sing, "the winds and the waves obey His will. Peace, be still. Peace, be still." The song and the passage speak of Christ's power over the natural elements. We read the story and sing without question. We trust that it happened, and trust that He could do it again. Yet, we would also say that we believe it easier for Jesus to calm a storm than calm our life. Teach teens to trust in the power than not only stills the troubled waters, but also stills our troubled souls.

5 **Jesus Raises a Stinky Man...He's Not Afraid of the Smell of Death** (John 11:1-54). Because of their youth, teens feel invincible and immortal. Death is a hard sell to those who seem to have so much life ahead of them. The "What then..." scenario helps young people take a small peek into their future. You know the drill. You ask a teen what they will do after high school. They respond by mentioning college or a career. You then ask, "What then?" You ask that question after every answer they give until the final response is "I guess after that I'll die." Let them know that Jesus is the only answer to the final "What then?"

6 **Jesus Used a Mountain as a Pulpit...He's the Master Teacher** (Matthew 5-7). Though teens might get tired of it, you could easily spend a year studying the Sermon on the Mount. Jesus covered everything from lust, to prayer, to hate, to building on the rock. The Lord knew how to take everyday emotions or actions and bring spiritual significance through them. Teach teens that Christ is still teaching from the mountain of their lives. Every locker has a lesson. Every bell could signify a wake up call.

**7 Jesus Cries...He's Got Heart** (Luke 13:34-35). Smart guy Jesus teaching in the synagogue. Wise guy Jesus outsmarting the Pharisees. Good guy Jesus healing the masses. Tough guy Jesus clearing out the temple. But sweet guy Jesus crying over a city? Our Lord gave the perfect picture of the perfect man. He knew when to be strong and when to release. When it came to sin we more often see Him sad than mad. His heart breaks with sin. His tears roll down His face as He sees His children turn away from Him.

**8 Jesus Catches Men...He's the Fisher of Men** (Mark 1:16-20). "Follow me." Do you feel you might have needed more than two words to tag along with a homeless teacher? Yet, twelve followed Him full time and countless others spent a great many hours with Him. The reason is not secret. He loved people. Jesus accepted them. They knew He was the one person they could approach who would have a non-judgmental attitude. Relay this picture of Jesus to your group so they can know that it's a life, not words, that leads others to the Father.



**9 Jesus Gives Sight to the Blind...He's the Light of the World** (John 9:1-7). After years of blindness the blind man learned about sight. After years of sin we finally learn about sight as well. The Lord shines His light to overcome the darkness in our hearts. He shines in our wide-open spaces and in the dark corners. He shines, hopefully, from the inside out so others can receive the gift of sight.

**10 Jesus Rises from the Dead...He's the Breath of Life** (Matthew 28:1-10). "In the beginning God said" (Genesis 1:1). Life comes from the breath of God. He speaks and it exists. The angel spoke, "Why do you seek the living among the dead?" That rhetorical question reveals the truth about Christ. He came so that we "might have life, and have it more abundantly" (John 10:10). Encourage the teens in your ministry to take a deep breath and exhale anything dead in their life. Have them take another deep breath and encourage them to feel Jesus' life enter them.

THIRTY EIGHT

# 10 Targets of Jesus' Ministry

1 **Palestine Population.** Jesus made it clear that He came to share the gospel with the lost sheep of Israel. He knew His exact target and the goal of His ministry. When we start getting geographically and demographically aquatinted with our communities we begin feeling like we are leaving people out. Instead look at this type of research as necessary. Without it you don't know who lives in your community and may never come to discover what it will take to reach them.

2 **Targeted Areas.** Jesus spent time in Galilee, Capernaum, Samaria, and other cities. His ministry grew because He went to a lot of different areas. Although He was sent to the lost sheep of Israel, He didn't limit His ministry.

We need to have a ministry at the church building, a ministry at the schools, a ministry at the ball games. If Jesus remained in one city all His life, his ministry would have been restricted. If we try to have everything at the building and are not willing to go out and meet people where they are, then our ministries will be limited.

3 **The Masses that Followed.** Almost everywhere Jesus went a crowd followed. Some followed out of curiosity. Some followed out of need. Some followed expecting a word from God. I'm sure that all received more than they anticipated. How do you develop a ministry that people

will follow? The same reason that people followed Jesus. Keep them curious. Provide healing, and give them God's word.

4 **His Friends.** Other than the twelve, Jesus hung out with Mary, Martha, and Lazarus more than anyone else. He appeared to be a regular at their house. Maybe He went there after an extended lesson. Perhaps it was His retreat center after a long week.

> Learn from Jesus' strategy and know your community and your people.

To make it in ministry we need friends. They help us refuel and get refocused. They protect us from the masses and help us meet the masses. Who are your friends? Ministry holds the potential to be a very lonely work without friends to share life with.

5 **The Religious.** Encounters with the religious became the Lord's most tense relationships. The Pharisees, Sadducees, teachers of the law, scribes, priests and other religious leaders formed an alliance against Jesus.

Don't think that the enemy won't use the religious to ruin your ministry. They wanted to stone Jesus and ultimately crucified him. They refused Judas' penance. And they did all of it in the name of God. Be prepared for the criticism, heartache, and challenges that come from those who call themselves your brothers and sisters.



6 **Individual Encounters.** The woman at the well, the woman caught in adultery, the blind man, and others all spent time with Jesus one on one. From the encounters we learn of Jesus' compassion, love, and heart for people.

Likewise, we need to spend one on one time with people. Howard Hendricks says, "You can impress people from a distance, but you can only impact them up close." For our ministry to have maximum impact we must get close to others.

7 **The Seventy Two.** "After this the Lord appointed seventy-two others and sent them two by two ahead of him to every town and place where he was about to go" (Luke

10:1). Out of all the masses that followed Him, the Lord chose seventy-two specifically. Their appointment means that Jesus had a ministry strategy. He didn't walk blindly into a harvest field without knowing the harvest. Sending the seventy-two is like asking a teen what their friends are like before you meet them. It's a way to discover the best way to approach someone so you don't waste time or make a foolish mistake.

8 **The Twelve.** The twelve are the best-known leadership team in the Bible. These men spent three years with Jesus as He prepared them to continue the ministry after His return to heaven. They were committed to leaving everything and following the Lord. While the seventy-two had a specific mission, they obviously didn't stay with Jesus all the time. You probably have teens that spend more time with you than other teens in the group. Consider them your twelve.

9 **The Three.** Peter, James, and John received more attention from Christ. They were there when Jesus was transfigured. They were closest to Jesus in the Garden of Gethsemene. Who are your dependable three? What are the names of the teens that you trust the most?

10 **The Apostle Jesus Loved.** "One of them, the disciple whom Jesus loved, was reclining next to him" (John 13:23). No offense to Peter and James, but Jesus loved John the most. That doesn't mean He played favorites. It means that John and His heart were the most alike. As you read His letters John speaks fervently about love. Maybe it's that characteristic that drew Christ to him. There is nothing wrong with loving a teen the most, just don't play favorites.

THIRTY NINE

# 10 Promotional Techniques

1 **Shoot a Video.** Let's say you need to promote an upcoming mission trip to Guatemala. Video tape a series of adventures using a couple of the teens as the missionaries. Part 1 could be "Pete and Re-Pete: Jungle Vines." Part 2 could be "Pete and Re-Pete in the Hot Seat." Because they are watching their peers it won't take much to make the videos funny and the scripts can be minimal. A four part series, four weeks out from sign up will work wonders.



2 **Enormous Banners.** Run a banner the length of your room and no one will be able to miss it. They can be made out of butcher paper, cloth, or if you have the money you can get them designed by a company. The last option is by far the most expensive and the most professional. Choose this option if you have the same event each year and you could reuse the banner time and time again. Otherwise a sheet of butcher paper, markers, and paint can't be beat.

3 **Count Down Clock.** Set the clock in a visible area of your youth room and constantly refer to it as the event nears. These large digital clocks can be used for all events, but using it for one big event a year might be best.

You can get a clock that counts down at countdown-clock.com, or by calling (516) 739-7800. Or if you have a computer in your room go online at http://www.toptips.com/Countdown.htm and get one there.

4 **Coupons.** Do you use early and late registrations for events? If so, consider using coupons. A coupon speaks of savings and although the amount saved would be the same without a coupon, the feeling of getting a deal will make some sign up early. You can take this concept to another level by getting scratch off games. One company to contact is Beachcliff graphics at http://www.beachcliffgraphics.com, or (440) 333-4300.

5 **Skits.** In order to promote a fund raising Sunday our church took "Have a Little Talk with Jesus" and rewrote the lyrics. The skit/song encouraged the church to give triple what they had ever given in one day. The skit took the edge off the concept of money and made the day a huge non-intimidating success. Drama or humorous skits hold a lot of power when it comes to creating a certain tone or atmosphere. Decide what emotion or instruction you want to deliver and go after it!



6 **Testimonies**. Personal experiences of a person go a long way in convincing others they need to become part of an event. When the group hears Tony talk about the life changing weekend last year's retreat turned out to be, it will encourage others to sign up. When Rita shares about the tears in the eyes of a physically challenged child at the children's hospital, others will want to receive the same blessing.

7 **Create a Catchy Title.** Get the group together and brainstorm for the best title imaginable. Don't go on a retreat; make it the "Expedition of San Pablo." Don't have a service project; have a "Towel and Basin" event. Since I'm not here brainstorming with anyone at the moment I couldn't come up with a really catchy title, but you get the idea.

8 **Newscasts.** Set up a corner of your youth room as the news center. Each

week have the news anchors broadcast information and exciting reports about the upcoming event. Invite the speaker, camp director, hospital advisors, or whoever will be involved in the occasion and have them join the crew for an interview segment.

> Whatever promotional technique you choose, begin using it early. Don't let great promo work fall apart because of poor timing.

9 **Wild Phone Tree or Email.** With the phone tree you could assemble a cast and read a script for the message. Each week send out a new phone tree message to the entire group.

With email you could write a short adventure piece each week leading up to the sign up. Always close the email with a cliffhanger that makes the teens want to read the next episode. Never make the reading more than about five minutes. If it's over three-quarters of a page chances are good they'll stop reading.

10 **Event Persona.** As mentioned in number eight bring in someone the teens will encounter on the trip, or event. Instead of doing a mock interview with a comedic news crew, play this out on a serious note. If the event is a mission trip then invite a local missionary in to tell about the do's and don'ts of the trip and the blessings they will get. If there is a regular missionary in your church, invite him or her to share with the class about their experiences.

## FORTY

# 10 Tips for When Your Own Teen Is in the Group

1 **Treat Him/Her the Same as Everyone Else.** When your own teen is part of the youth group it's tempting to hold him/her to a higher standard. "Don't embarrass me" comments come from parent and teen. Being singled out is a child's fear.

Don't treat your teen any different than anyone else's teen. Give the same amount of space. Expect the same behavior and respect. Try to only be their youth minister unless it's absolutely necessary to become a parent.

2 **Give Them Options**. Just because they are your child doesn't mean they want to be on the leadership team. It doesn't mean they want to go on the retreat. It doesn't mean they want to wake up at 5 a.m. on Saturday morning to get ready for a service project. Encourage but don't force your teen to do anything he/she doesn't want to do. We all know that the end result of unwilling obedience is rejection and rebellion.

3 **Give Them Money Before the Trip.** By doing this you will provide some independence. If she wants more money she'll come ask you. But if she has to get money from you at every stop it will appear like her dad is on the trip. No one else in the group is having to rely on mom and dad for funds, she shouldn't have to either.

4 **Never Get in a Power Struggle in Front of the Group.** "I'm your father and you will do what I say!" At the moment everyone in the group is watching to see who is in charge. If your son smarts back and you relent then he appears to have the upper hand. If you force him back with your parental rights then you have shown who the boss is. Either way you are both losers. Chances are above average that the group will feel sorry for your son and angry at you. If a difficulty arises handle everything in private.

5 **Phone Home.** When you are out making your weekly visits or attending a conference, call home to talk to your teens. Keeping in touch will let them know that they are important to you. It's critical that your children know that you love them more than anyone else in the group. Although you treat them the same in public, and provide some space, they need to know that deep down they matter. With all the time we spend with everybody else's children, it would be easy for our own teen to feel left out and neglected.



6 **Mail Outs.** Don't save the postage and bring the youth group mail-out home with you. Let your kids get the information in the mail. It's just another way of saying, "I consider you part of the group." It helps them have their own identity. On the other hand if you come home and they say, "Hey dork, why don't you just bring it home with you and save the postage?" that's a good sign that a mail-out is not essential.

7 **Encouraging Notes.** Send at least one note a month to your teen encouraging him/her to stay strong and focused. Encourage her spiritually to be all that God designed. Encourage him to always follow God's will regardless of the situation. Use these notes as a way to let your teen know how much he/she means to you and how much you desire them to thrive in their faith.

8 **Be Careful of Including Your Teen in Illustrations.** Get permission every time from your teen before you use her in an illustration. You might think the story is cute, but she might feel it is humiliating. You might think the account makes your son look like a hero, but he might think it makes him look like an idiot. This is one case when it is easier to get permission than forgiveness.

9 **Don't Take Your Frustrations Out on Your Teen.** So the youth group is uncommitted, irresponsible, and worldly, using your teen as an emotional punching bag will do no good. Your child is one teen in the group, not the entire group. If we let out our hurts on our kids then they will assume that we feel that they are to blame for the situation. They will feel that the success or failure of the group is directly tied to them.

10 **Pray.** Let your teen know that you are praying for him/her. Better yet, spend time each day praying together. Let him know that he is part of your team. Let her know that she is indispensable to the group. Pray that God will use both of you in a unique way for His glory and the group's growth.

Forty One

# 10 Devotional Guides and Workbooks

1 **My Utmost for His Highest.** The most popular devotional guide ever written. It is available in a variety of styles from straight text to updated language. Choose the best style for your study. We recommend the Oswald Chambers' classic, best-selling devotional in the handy, loose-leaf format. Updated edition in today's language, edited by James Reimann. An entry for every day of the year. Each page will challenge you to give your very best to the Savior.

Author: Oswald Chambers. Publisher: Moody Press ISBN: 0802427863

2 **Experiencing God.** Learn to hear when God is speaking to you. Authors Blackaby and King encourage you to find out where God is working in the world around you so that you can join Him. A workbook that will change your life, *Experiencing God* will lead you in an exploration of the seven vital aspects of your relationship with God: knowing, loving, hearing, joining, believing, obeying and experiencing.

Authors: Henry Blackaby & Claude King. Publisher: Broadman/Holman ISBN: 0805499547

3 **Life in the Spirit.** See the Holy Spirit in Scripture and in your life. Examine how the Spirit designed you with specific purpose. Watch as the Spirit of God reveals to you. Learn what the Holy Spirit is doing in the world to-

day. Discover how you can live a Spirit-filled life. Experience the power of the Spirit as you study during this 13 week course.

Author: Robertson McQuilken Publisher: Lifeway ISBN: 0767325869

4 **Following God.** This is a series of five workbooks built around the theme of following God. They provide a look at the lives of key characters found in the Bible. The theme emphasizes the importance of developing a relationship with God and living a life totally surrendered to His leading. Examples are given of those who received blessings from their walk with God as well as the stories of those who refused to follow Him completely. The characters are viewed from a historical perspective and we are given interesting facts regarding the time in which these figures lived.

Authors: Various. Publisher: AMG



5 **The Mind of Christ.** To be like Jesus! That is why God created us. *The Mind of Christ* will challenge you to think the thoughts of Jesus – to have the very mind of Christ as commanded in Philippians 2:5. There is no doubt that we all need to acquire the thinking of our Lord as we seek to mature and become like Him.

Authors: T.W. Hunt and Claude V. King. Publishers: Lifeway ISBN: 085498702

6 **The Heart of the Problem.** Twelve detailed chapters divided into five daily lessons. *The Heart of the Problem* does a great service to those who would seek God's guidance. Brandt and Skinner call it like it is and state that a majority of our difficulties are a direct result of sin. This workbook is a call to holiness that convicts without condemning.

Authors: Henry Brandt and Kerry L. Skinner. Publisher: Broadman/Holman ISBN: 0805416676

7 **Charles R. Swindoll Study Guides.** Chuck Swindoll is a favorite author and speaker of many Christians. His daily radio program *Insight for Living*, provides practical

and encouraging messages. Free study guides are available from the program which coincides with the present study. However, all of Swindoll's guides are available and are too many to list here. You can write Insight for Living at P.O. Box 69000, Anaheim, CA 92817-0900. Or call 1-800-772-8888. Kay Arthur is another popular Bible study guide provider.

8 **When God Speaks.** The format of the course is simple. The major ways God speaks to His people are covered in six weeks. Each daily lesson takes about 15 to 20 minutes, but when God speaks to you, you will want to continue to listen. The goal is to genuinely experience God's presence in your daily life.

Authors: Henry and Richard Blackaby. Publisher: Lifeway. ISBN: 0805498222

9 **Jesus On Leadership, Student Edition.** This workbook covers seven principles of servant leadership. Your youth group and your church will benefit from a leadership that is based on serving rather than being served. We recommend the student edition because you may want to do this study with your group. Also, many studies that are written on a teen level tend to be perfect for adults.

Author: C. Gene Wilkes Publisher: Lifeway. ISBN: 0767394879

10 **The Blessing.** What the Bible calls "the blessing" is a life-changing acceptance that heals and brings inner peace. We all long for it from our parents and we all can bestow it on others. This practical, interactive workbook helps you understand and apply the five principles of the blessing. As you walk through this personal journey, you'll discover the roots of family acceptance, overcome rejection from the past, and learn to pass the blessing on.

Authors: Gary Smalley and John Trent, Ph.D. Publisher: Thomas Nelson/Word. ISBN: 0840745559

FORTY TWO

# 10 Techniques to Minister to Single Parents

1 **Read the Baker Handbook of Single Parent Ministry.** Bringing together the insight of twenty-eight seasoned leaders from the Network of Single Adult Leaders (NSL), this comprehensive handbook addresses the challenges faced by single parents - including the never married, the widowed, and the divorced. This handbook provides fourteen types of ministry churches can use to respond to the needs of single parents and their children. Although this information is for those seeking to start a single parent ministry, you can use this information to respond to the needs of your single parents. ISBN 0801090520

2 **Bible Wisdom for Single Parents.** This small book is only around $2 so it would make a great gift for the single parents in your ministry. Loneliness, guilt, economic and social pressures often seem insurmountable to a single raising children. *Bible Wisdom for Single Parents* provides Scriptures for all the emotions and struggles they are facing. ISBN 0781400724

3 **Friday Night Out.** Single parents rarely get a break. In a two-parent household one spouse can keep the kids while the other takes some time alone. Not so with a single parent. They have to handle every responsibility alone. It's not that they don't have friends, they just don't

want to feel like a burden to them. Every other month or so let the teens provide free child care for all the single parents of your church even if they don't have teens in the group. The single parents you build relationships with now will be the same ones you work with when their kids reach youth group age.

4 **Articles.** As you read the newspaper, magazines, and other materials, cut out any articles that relate to single parenting that would be helpful. Keep a folder and collect for a month. Then take the articles and photo copy them and send them out to the single parents of the teens in your group. Some articles will be right on target and some won't relate at all, but that's alright because they will know that you care and consider them as part of your ministry.

5 **Be Terminology Conscious.** It's easy to assume dual parent relationships and always say things like, "Make sure your mom and dad come this Saturday to the meeting." Immediately the teens with only one parent in the home will feel distanced. You don't need to rework your entire vocabulary, just be inclusive of single parent families. Sometimes say, "Your mom or your dad." A word as simple as "or" instead of "and" can prove that you are aware and sensitive.

6 **Know the Facts.** In the past twenty-five years, the number of single parent families has more than doubled. According to U.S. Census Bureau estimates, 59 percent of United States children will live in a single-parent home at least once during their minor years. That is a majority. Over 16 million children currently live in single-parent homes. More and more of these families can be defined as "binuclear" families, with both parents actively involved in parenting and creating two separate homes for their children. Divorce and remarriage, rather than being the exception, are more and more common in families today.

7 **Support.** You may decide to reach out to single parents by providing a support group or small group to meet their needs. *Just Me and the Kids, Divorce Care*, and *Grief Recovery* are the most popular Christian support formats available. If your church does not have the ability or funds to provide this type of support, contact area churches and refer your single parents to their group which probably meets on a non-service night.

8 **Financial Advice.** *The Financial Guide for the Single Parents* by Larry Burkett provides step by step monetary planning for the single parent. Offer this book as a resource to help single income families get a grip on their money. Larry's organization, *Christian Financial Concepts*, excels in biblical principles for stewardship.

9 **Singles Supper.** Invite the single parents and their teens over to your place for supper. (If you're single and you only have one single parent of the opposite sex forget this tip). You can invite a few over at a time, or have a banquet at the church and host all. Don't use this as a time to make single parents feel degraded or singled out. Use this as a time to honor them for their commitment to their family despite the obstacles.



10 **Fresh Start**. There's no way around it-divorce is a terribly painful experience for everyone involved. In this practical workbook, family experts Burns and Whiteman offer compassionate counsel to those facing this trauma. They've included Bible-based guidelines and legal and financial advice, as well as dozens of exercises to help the recently divorced begin the healing process. *Fresh Start Divorce Recovery Workbook*, ISBN: 0785271929

FORTY THREE

# 10 P's of Successful Youth Ministry

1 **Purpose.** "Whatever you do in word or deed do all to the glory of God" (Colossians 3:17). Regardless of who you are trying to reach or the format type you adopt, everything should point directly back to God. There should be a biblical purpose behind each activity whether it's labeled social or spiritual.



2 **Prayer.** "Worry about nothing, pray about everything" (Philippians 4:6). Do we really pray about everything? Do we spend as much time in prayer over a two hour service project as we do a three day retreat? As we pray we are asking God to do what He wouldn't have done had we not asked. Don't we want that in every area of our ministry? Let's rub some holes in our jeans from our knees hitting the floor.

3 **Plan.** "For which of you before he builds a tower, does not sit down first and count the cost, whether he has enough to finish it?" (Luke 14:28). As stated in 10 X 50 – a goal without a plan is nothing more than a wish. God had a plan with Noah, Abraham, Moses, Joshua and on and on and on. The Father honors a plan that honors Him. A plan proves that we feel the event is worth the effort, while the lack of a plan can show apathy or laziness.

**4 Personal.** "And when Jesus went out and saw the great multitude, He was moved with compassion for them and healed their sick" (Matthew 14:14). That verse and many others like it is why we call Him our personal Savior. Even in a crowd Jesus touched the individual. Our ministries should reflect Jesus' personal style. We should touch each teen where they need love and acceptance. Because of their attendance or willingness to serve we are going to spend more time with more teens than others, but not one should get neglected or ignored.

**5 Perfection.** "Therefore, be perfect as your heavenly Father is perfect (Matthew 5:48). When this verse is read I always hear the disclaimer, "Jesus was using a hyperbole in this verse. We can't expect to be perfect." Both of those statements may be true, but that shouldn't stop us from making an attempt at perfection. If we never put perfection on the list, we will never make it. Strive for excellence above and beyond the average ministry.

**6 Power.** "For the kingdom is not of talk, but of power" (1 Corinthians 4:20). Do we talk more about what we are going to do, or about what God is going to do? Whatever we choose to do will be limited. Whatever God chooses to do will be unlimited. When God's power is present in the ministry there's no need for big talk because we have an Almighty God. The power that split the Red Sea, turned water into wine, and raised the dead is available to us today, so let's talk soft and carry a big God.

**7 Preach.** "Preach the word in all seasons" (2 Timothy 4:2). Sometimes you need to teach and sometimes we need to preach. We need to be able to lay it on the line without a parable, or an object lesson, or a clever story. There are times when we want the group to discover the lesson for themselves and times when we need to make it painfully clear so no one can walk away without understanding. Preaching is a traditional term that we often leave for the guy who stands behind the pulpit. Dust it off and put it into practice. You don't have to tell the teens you're preaching - just do it when it's necessary.

8 **Passion.** "...His word was in my heart like a burning fire shut up in my bones. I am weary of holding it in, and indeed I cannot" (Jeremiah 20:9). That's passion. It's an internal flame that cannot be extinguished, instead it must be released. Passion longs for all that God will give. It hungers for all that God can fill. It overflows with unquenchable emotion. When our ministries contain passion no one will remain untouched by God's desire.

9 **Propriety.** "Be holy for I am holy" (1 Peter 1:16). Holiness should be a mark of our ministry. Every word and action is measured against the standard of holiness. Holiness should determine what the teens wear, where they go, what movies they watch in the hotel room after the day's events, etc. Many youth groups resemble the world with only the name of Christ attached to them. A standard of propriety will produce a walk in Christ, not just a claim of Christ (1 John 2:6).

10 **Praise.** "Therefore let us offer continually to God the sacrifice of praise, the fruit of our lips giving praise to His name" (Hebrews 13:15). Let God's praises ring through your group. Praise God through singing and sharing. Lift Him up with words of adoration and thanksgiving. Give Him the glory and honor for every blessing. If we're breathing, we should be praising (Psalm 150:6).

FORTY FOUR

# 10 Questions

1 **What is the number one priority in your life?**



2 **What are you working on that makes a difference?**

3 **How has God gifted you and how are you using those gifts?**

4 **If you could add one skill or talent to your life what would it be and why?**

5 **Where would you like to be in three years? five years? ten years? twenty years?**

6 **What is preventing you from reaching God's vision for your life?**

Use the space provided to answer these questions, or use a separate sheet. Don't rush through this exercise. Pray and meditate on each question.

How will you allow the answers to these questions to change your life?

7 **What words do you like to hear most?**

8 **If you had only one month to live, how would you live it?**

9 **If your friends were to describe you to someone else what would they say?**

10 **How do you want to be remembered?**

## FORTY FIVE

# 10 TOOLS FOR VISION CASTING

**Verify the Source.** Did the desire come from God or from you? Moses knew the vision was from God. Abraham knew the vision was from God. Paul knew the vision was from God. Nehemiah knew the vision was from God.

Is it a good idea or a God idea? Use the tools on page 111 to help you determine the source of the vision.

**Inspiring.** Does the vision make you want to move? Moses' vision made him want to stay put, while Abraham's vision literally made him move. The shared vision should result in action. It should create energy and the desire of not resting until the vision becomes reality.

**Scriptural.** Does the vision correlate with God's will? One of the most innocent ways we can cast a less than scriptural vision is by exalting our name. For example, we may decide on making the name of our group known throughout the city, so when youth ministry is mentioned our group is mentioned. That sounds like a great goal, but it that God's will? Does He want our name to be known or His name to be know? That may appear picky or walking a fine line, but don't we think that the Lord wants every vision to match with Scripture?

**Instruction.** Details of how to accomplish the vision should coincide with proclaiming the vision. We are only giving a pep talk if we ignite the heart with a lot of ideas that have no formula. Jesus told the apostles to "Go into all the world and make disciples, baptizing them in the name of the Father and of the Son and of the Holy Spirit. Teaching them to obey everything I have commanded you for I am with your always, even until the very end of the age" (Matthew 28:19-20). The Lord cast the vision and told them how to accomplish it.

**Often.** Without sounding like a skipping CD, regularly restate the vision. The Hebrews writer challenges us to "fix your eyes on Jesus, the author and finisher of our faith" (Hebrews 12:2). When we lose sight of the goal we get distracted and discouraged.

**Need.** Does the vision fill a void? There's no need to form and cast a vision just to say your ministry has one. The result of the statement should fill an emptiness, heal a heart, connect a community, or anything along the lines of a need.



**Change.** Will lives be changed? Hundreds of books have been written on making successful changes. They talk about how reluctant people are to change and how difficult it is to get some people to change. The strength of a well crafted vision statement is that it makes people want to change. Teens and parents are not against change as long as it's a proven need. A vision that results in closer family relationships or a deeper walk with God, will be welcomed. Those accepting the vision would understand a cost is involved but will be willing to pay because the end result promises a changed life.

**Alive.** Does the vision need dusting? We created a vision statement for our group that sounded great. All the leaders were excited and we knew we had a God vision that would take the ministry to the next level for the Lord. Unfortunately, a year later nothing had really happened with the statement. It contained all the right elements and we repeated it often, but it just died. Learn from my experience, recasting a dead vision is worthless.

**Sharpen.** Is there uncertain or needless wording? A vision should be tight and clearly understood by all. God said to Noah, "Build and ark and do it like this." When God finished sharing the vision with Noah, he didn't say, "Um, Lord, what are you talking about?"

**Thirst.** Do people feel like they can't live without the vision? "Without a vision the people perish" (Proverbs 29:18). The literal translation means that without a word from God people waste away. A God-sized vision will call for His refreshing of a parched life.

> "VISION IS BORN IN THE HEART OF THE MAN AND WOMAN WHO IS CAUGHT BETWEEN THE TENSION OF WHAT COULD BE AND WHAT SHOULD BE."
> - ANDY STANLEY, VISIONEERING.

FORTY SIX

# 10 Newsletter Tips

1 **Layout.** Make it clean and easy to read. That sounds simple, but most newsletters look cluttered and disorganized. If you're using a desktop publishing program begin with one of their predesigned templates and adapt it to your needs.

Get copies of other youth group newsletters to see how other groups go about design. Take the best, ignore the worst, and make improvements. You don't have to be a graphic artist to create a tidy newsletter.

2 **Fonts.** Some rules suggest never using more than three different fonts in a newsletter. We suggest doing whatever looks the best. If you only need one, then use one. If you need ten, then use ten. They key to cool fonting is choosing lettering that matches the messages and the clipart. You might choose "x-files" font for a resurrection story, but using the same font for birthday announcements might not get it.

Looking for fonts? Any local software store will have a bundle. If you don't want to pay, then logon to your favorite search engine and type in "free fonts." You'll never run out of fonts again.

**3 Articles.** Write a short, concise, thought for the month (if this is a monthly publication). Pick a text and provide challenging insight and applicable points.

Collecting submissions from the youth group will increase newsletter reading. Perhaps the group members will read your article. It's almost guaranteed that they will at least skim a peer's work.

**4 Calendar.** A calendar is a listing of events that clearly details upcoming activities. Another name for calendar is "the most ignored and least read page of the newsletter." *Really?* Yep, because you'll notice that teens and parents are calling you all the time to find out what you have already provided on the calendar. *Then why do one?* Because at least one family will appreciate it.

**5 Pictures.** Got some zany photos from the lock-in? Paste them. Got some incriminating baby snapshots? Post them. Teens act embarrassed when they see their picture, but there is no one else they would rather look at than themselves. So be liberal with the images if you have the space. (Speaking of space, you probably want to go with 11" x 17" folded in half if you want plenty of room.)

**6 Spotlight.** Highlight a teen or two each month. Supply a picture and tell their birthday, hobbies, favorite food, most embarrassing moment, etc.

**7 Review.** Have a teen write a review of a Christian book they have read or their favorite Christian music. Ask them to share the pros and cons of the material and a basic recommendation. Reviews can be fun with a loose cannon in the group vowing to "never spend my hard earned coins for such a stinky band again!"

8 **Clipart.** Church Art Works has almost a dozen clipart books out with great images for youth ministry. It is also available on CD-ROM. Again, you can logon and search for free clipart and get all you will ever need. The only problem is that you will have to sort through a lot of junk before you find any suitable material. Only use images with a high DPI (dots per inch) resolution, otherwise you will get grainy art that no printer or program can adjust.

9 **Passages.** Place Bible verses strategically throughout the newsletter. You can use them to separate topics and events instead of using lines. To offset them more, draw a box around them so they are distinct from the rest of the text. When using Scripture just make sure the passage makes sense. That means no archaic language and no genealogies.

**To catch a reader's attention put a passage in a box like this in your newsletter.**

10 **Interview.** A simple question and answer format always works. Before a big retreat, interview someone who went last year. Before a mission trip, interview a member of the church who has been on a mission trip. Better yet, write to the area you will visit and let a local fill out the interview, then the teens will look forward to meeting their long distance interview.

## FORTY SEVEN

# 10 Tips for Teen Dating Relationships

**1 The Standard.** "[3]It is God's will that you should be sanctified: that you should avoid sexual immorality; [4]that each of you should learn to control his own body in a way that is holy and honorable, [5]not in passionate lust like the heathen, who do not know God;" (1 Thessalonians 4:3-5). That answers every question of "how far is too far." If an action is not holy and honorable then it's out of bounds. Let teens know that Scripture says we cannot participate in anything we would not be willing to share every minute detail about after the date.



**2 Set Limits.** "...but as for me and my household, we will serve the LORD" (Joshua 24:15). Teens should let their dates know upfront exactly what to expect, and not to expect. There's nothing wrong with a girl saying, "I want to be honest with you. If you are going out with me because you think something is going to happen, you need to know it's not."

**3 Accountability.** "When the apostles returned, they reported to Jesus what they had done..." (Luke 9:10). Encourage the group members to select at least one person they call after every date. Accountability only works if the person will be true to the relationship. That means he or she must give a full account of the date even if unholy actions took place. Sharing with another person will allow the teen to stay stronger because of knowing the upcoming conversation. It will also aid the healing process if things didn't go as planned or help the hope process when things did.

4 **Remember a Passage.** "[9]How can a young man keep his way pure? By living according to your word. [10]I seek you with all my heart; do not let me stray from your commands. [11]I have hidden your word in my heart that I might not sin against you." (Psalm 119: 9-11). God's words act as a guard against sin. Select about ten passages that you feel relate to teen dating and print them on a sheet for your group.

5 **Date a Committed Believer.** "Do not be yoked together with unbelievers. For what do righteousness and wickedness have in common? Or what fellowship can light have with darkness?" (2 Corinthians 6:14). Does that verse absolutely forbid non-Christian dating? Not necessarily, but it does show the foolishness involved in becoming deeply involved with someone with no faith. Why would a Christian want to date a non-Christian anyway?



6 **Test the Love** (1 Corinthians 13). There's not room to print the entire chapter, but you know it well. Whenever a teen starts talking about love, have them put it to the test. Is their love pure? Is it out of respect? Does it put the other person first? Too many young people have fallen into the trap of, "If you love me you will." As the popular resource says, "True love waits."

7 **Wear Running Shoes.** "Flee from sexual immorality. All other sins a man commits are outside his body, but he who sins sexually sins against his own body" (1 Corinthians 6:18). It's better to run than to succumb. Maybe your group won't go

around quoting that slogan, but the principle is true. Most teens will think it's corny to ask to be taken home or to literally get out and start walking. Joseph, however, knew it was better to run than to sin against God (Genesis 39:1-12).

8 **Remain Visible.** "Everyone who does evil hates the light, and will not come into the light for fear that his deeds will be exposed. [21]But whoever lives by the truth comes into the light, so that it may be seen plainly that what he has done has been done through God" (John 3:20-21). It's rare that you spot a teen sinning on a date in public. Don't they try to hide it? Don't they look for a dark parking areas, or an empty house? Share with the group the importance of always being visible on a date.

9 **Talk Openly About God.** "But in your hearts set apart Christ as Lord. Always be prepared to give an answer to everyone who asks you to give the reason for the hope that you have" (1 Peter 3:15). Peter writes through the Spirit that we are to "always be prepared." By setting their hearts apart for God's purposes, teens can clearly communicate the purposes for which they have been set apart.

10 **Remember Whose You Are.** "Do you not know that your body is a temple of the Holy Spirit, who is in you, whom you have received from God? You are not your own; [20]you were bought at a price. Therefore honor God with your body" (1 Corinthians 6:19-20). The blood of Jesus paid the price for sin. That reason alone should be enough to keep us strong. Remind teens that they too have been purchased by the blood of Christ.

FORTY EIGHT

# 10 Techniques for Inner City Ministry

**1 Do Take a Genuine Interest in the Inner City Residents.** The inner city may be considered the projects, but they don't want to be a project. If they get the feeling that your group thinks they are poor people looking for a handout you may never be able to make a lasting impact. Show that you care about each person by making eye contact and listening attentively as they share their heartaches and dreams.

**2 Do Get to Know them on a First Name Basis.** Have teens introduce themselves and listen closely to the name of the individual they are speaking with. If your group is working with the inner city of your town this will be a valuable tool as you revisit. The next time you are ministering in the area and you are able to greet the residents on a first name basis, you will have proven that you care about them as people.

**3 Do Work in Teams.** Never allow any teen to enter a

home or even knock on a door alone. All groups need to have three members and each group needs at least one male. Few groups have reported anything other than inappropriate comments being made, but you never know what could occur. Take precaution by keeping your teens in groups and telling them to be alert.

4 **Do Report All Problems to Inner City Staff or Team Leaders.** If a resident male is making advances on the girls, or if a drug deal is going down, report it. The staff is not the police and will not be able to handle it that way, but they do know the community and will know what steps to take. If you are new to this particular ministry ask the leaders to make your teens aware of the average encounters they may expect.

5 **Do Relax, Have Fun, and Enjoy the Blessing of Serving.** Most of the residents are friendly, loving, and excited that someone wants to help them get closer to God. One of the best areas will be working with the children. They are fun and thrilled that you have come to play with them.



6 **Don't Wear Clothes or Jewelry that Will Draw Attention.** Make it extremely clear to your girls that they will not wear anything revealing or alluring. Most ministries advise the teens to wear long pants and not shorts or tank tops or halter tops.

Expensive jewelry is also discouraged because some of the residents may see your teens as a way to get their next drug fix, or make their next car payment. Some may approach and say, "Gimme that necklace." Avoid confrontation by leaving the gold at home.

7 **Don't Point and Stare at Anyone.** Teens are notorious for making their emotions evident to all. If they see

someone strung out on crack or drunk and they start staring and pointing the individual may approach them. Other residents in the community will be embarrassed and feel they are just a sideshow for your group.

8 **Don't Give Out Candy, Gifts, Food, or Clothing without Permission from the Inner City Leadership.** The local ministry has worked hard at getting the people to accept Jesus, not charity. Inner City worker Jonathan Moseby says, "When they get gifts from you they are harder to reach because they will say what you want to hear in order to receive the next gift."

9 **Don't Enter Any Homes or Apartments**. Several groups should be within eyesight of each other at all times. Tell your teens that no matter how sweet someone appears they are not to enter the home. When invited to come in have them say, "Thank you anyway, but we need to go to the next house." Leave whatever materials you are handing out with the person, then move on.



10 **Don't Approach Large Groups of People without the Inner City Leadership Present.** When large groups are hanging out together in the community there may be a drug deal occurring. Instruct your teens to stay clear of these groups and do not go near them even if they say they want to see what you are handing out.

FORTY NINE

# 10 More Quiet Time Tools

When time is pressing don't cancel your time with God. Use one of these quiet time suggestions to meditate on the Lord. They're simple, yet powerful: Read the Passage, sing a song of praise in response, and pray for the Father to instill the principle in your life.



1 **Principle:**Give Thanks to the Lord.
**Passage:** Psalm 105:1-4
**Praise:** "Thank You Lord" by Dennis Jernigan
**Prayer:** *Father, I thank you for remembering me on the cross. Thank you for taking my sin debt away. Thank you for being faithful even in the midst of my unfaithfulness.*

2 **Principle:** God Places a Song within Us
**Passage:** Ephesians 5:15-20
**Praise:** "In Moments Like These" by David Graham
**Prayer:** *Father, thank you for the song of my life. May others hear your music through my actions. May the orchestra you created in my heart be displayed through my deeds. May the words of my mouth become lyrics in the heavens.*

3 **Principle:** Jesus, the Savior of All
**Passage:** Luke 2:1-20
**Praise:** "A Wonderful Savior" by Fanny & Kirkpatrick
**Prayer:** *Father, your gift of the Savior is indescribable. The angels sang. The shepherds worshiped. May the Savior be reborn in the stable of my heart. May there always be room.*

4 **Principle:** God is Exalted
**Passage:** 2 Samuel 22:47-51
**Praise:** "He is Exalted" by Twila Paris
**Prayer:** *Father, you are above all else. It is just as you said, your ways are not our ways. Your thoughts are above our thoughts. I exalt you Father for your love. I exalt you Father for your grace. I exalt you and place you above all others in my life.*

5 **Principle:** God Delivers
**Passage:** Psalm 18
**Praise:** "I Will Call Upon the Lord" by Michael O'Shields
**Prayer:** *Father, I call on your great name for protection against those who would harm me. Grant me strength and power in weakness. Deliver me from sin and shield me from temptation.*

6 **Principle:** God's Greatness
**Passage:** Exodus 3:13-22
**Praise:** "How Great Thou Art" by Stuart K. Hine
**Prayer:** *Father, why do I continue to try to do everything myself? Why do I worry about how I will look to others, or whether or not the task will be completed? Prove to me, like Moses, that it is You who is in control, not me.*

7 **Principle:** The Goodness of God's Presence
**Passage:** Psalm 23
**Praise:** "I Want to be Where you are" by Don Moen
**Prayer:** *Father, I want to be in your presence each moment. Wrap my life with your glory. Let me feel you beside me both at work and play. May you become as real to me as the people I walk with day by day. May we walk together like you and Enoch. May we talk together like you and Moses.*

8 **Principle:** Seeing Myself in the Picture of the Cross
**Passage:** Matthew 27:11-28:20
**Praise:** "When I Survey the Wondrous Cross" by Watts & Chant
**Prayer:** *Father, though the cross should have been mine thank you for giving Christ my place. Forgive me for the times I have driven nails through his hands and feet. Give me spiritual vision so I can understand the significance of Calvary and honor you accordingly.*

9 **Principle:** Praise for God's Mighty Works
**Passage:** Habakkuk 3:2
**Praise:** "Blessed Be the Lord God Almighty" by Bob Fitts
**Prayer:** *Father, show yourself powerful in my life. Be known as a God who does, not a God who did. Thank you for the testimony of your power through the transformations in my heart. Continue your mighty works in me through the power of your Spirit.*

10 **Principle:** Priceless Redemption
**Passage:** 1 Peter 1:18-19
**Praise:** "I Am Mine No More" - unknown
**Prayer:** *Father, thank you for the priceless gift. Thank you for not redeeming me with silver and gold but by the blood of the Lamb. You are my King, I am your servant. I praise you for making me like Jesus.*

FIFTY

# 10 Common Criticisms

And How to Deal with Them.

**1** **You Only Spend Time with Your Favorites.** This complaint usually comes from a parents whose child is not involved. Since there is nothing wrong with their child there is obviously something wrong with you.

Tip: Look at a list of the teens in your group and take an honest evaluation. Are there teens you spend more time with than others? Is it because they are favorites or because they happen to be present? Are there any in the group you purposely ignore? Talk with the parent about your time and why you feel their child is or isn't getting the attention they desire.

**2** **Your Classes Are Boring and Unprepared**. Has the parent that makes the complaint actually been in your class? If not then consider the student. Does he or she pay attention?

Tip: Prepare and present the best class you can. Every teacher is not going to be the best in the world, but that's all right. As long as we are not intentionally unprepared or boring we can't be faulted. We only try to become the best we are able to be.

**3** **You are Too Involved in Outside Interests.** This complaint can surface when you participate with some teens on a level that others can't. For example, let's say you love rafting and you have some in the group that love it. Parents of teens who have children who don't like rafting will find fault and say you do too much fun stuff.

Tip: Remain balanced and make sure everyone is invited to everything. Just because a hobby can become a ministry tool does not mean you have to feel guilty.

**4** **You Are Paid Too Much for the Work You Do.** When someone says that you can say, "Have you seen my check lately?" I am usually tempted to say, "What's the worth of a soul?" Neither approach works very well.

Tip: You can ignore the comment or prove him or her wrong. If they want, they can sit down with you and you can outline an average week. Chances are good that by the end of the conversation they'll admit that you do more than they do in the average week. Plus you will have a supporter that no one can shake.



**5** **You Don't Keep the Parents Informed.** Don't rely on teens to get the handout or information to their parents.

Tip: Mail each parent a copy of everything you hand the teens regarding events or trips. If a parent receives a personal copy, then a complaint can't be justified.

**6** **You Never Visit Our Home.** Believe it or not some parents actually want an in home visit from you. They take it personally if you visit any other family at home and don't visit theirs.

Tip: Make it known that you are more than willing to visit any family that desires one. Place it on the family's shoulders to call you and set up a time. Let families know that you might feel like you are imposing if you call and set up an appointment. Instead let them make the invitation.

**7** **You're Too Young and Immature to Take Our Teens on a Trip.** Of course, mainly young youth ministers hear the young part, while we all may hear the immature aspect.

Tip: Is there any reason for the complaint? Has youth and immaturity been a factor in the past? If not, then point to your record. Also, having parental chaperones on the trip will counter parental arguments. But it is important for your adult chaperones to understand who will be in charge on the trip.

8 **You Over Schedule the Teens.** The summers are filled with this complaint.

Tip: Again, remain balanced. This is a tough area because if you do too little then parents complain, and if you do too much, parents complain.

9 **You Try to Make Too Many Changes.** Youth culture is very different from the generation of their parents. Parents may see this as a threat to their doctrine and feel that you are trying to "change the church."

Tip: Emphasize the importance of change. The reason Christ came is so we would be changed into His image. Always link your change in method or style to a biblical principle. If parents can see a righteous reason for the shift, they are more likely to accept it.

10 **We Don't See Our Teens Growing Spiritually**. Another way this is stated is, "You guys play all the time."

Tip: Let parents know that spiritual maturity takes time to develop. The seeds planted today may not be seen for many seasons. Also, gently remind the parents that youth ministry is to supplement the spiritual training of the home, not supercede it.

FIFTY ONE

# 10 Techniques for Rewarding Volunteers

**1 Say Thank You.** Next to "I love you," "thank you" are the most longed for words. There are many ways to say these words, but don't forget calls and cards. A thirty-second phone conversation can change the outlook of someone's day. A smile will cross her face when she learns how much you appreciate her. A letter with a couple of lines of gratitude will let him know that his effort isn't going unnoticed. 

**2 Free Lunch.** People say there's no free lunch, but there will be for your volunteers when you take them. If possible, get a budget line approved for volunteer meals and take a couple out each month. During your time together share some of the things that have impressed you most with their service. Let them know specifically the impact they have had on the group.

**3 Youth Group Appreciation Party.** Form a youth committee and plan a party for the volunteers. Have various teens tell about the volunteer that has meant the most to him or her. Make sure each volunteer has a young person that shares. The party can consist of finger foods and games. So for one night your workers get to be served rather than serve.

**4 Cover Their Youth Trip Costs.** Volunteers not only give their time; they give their cash. Working for free can cost some people a lot of money. Help keep some weight in their wallets and pocket books by paying for part of their expenses on youth trips. You may want to pay for some meals, the hotel room, or the conference cost. Anything you can pay for will be appreciated.

**5 Extra-mile Award.** Honor your volunteers in front of your group and in front of your church. On youth Sunday, or any Sunday you can get permission, give an extra-mile award to those who serve in your ministry. Point out to the congregation the amount of time and focus necessary to be a volunteer in your ministry.

**6 Video Scrapbook.** Gather all the photos and videos you can from the teens. Out of the material get the best of the best and make a video collage. Use still shots by placing them upright on a counter and zooming in so no edges are in view. Video for about five seconds then press pause. Repeat the process until all the photos have been used. As you transfer to a VHS tape you can run an audio wire from your CD player to the back of your VCR and pipe in some background music. Give copies to your volunteers so they can have a unique reminder of their service.

**7 Gift Certificate.** Do a survey and ask your volunteers to write down their favorite places to eat, their favorite stores, and their favorite brands. With that information in hand you are ready to purchase a gift certificate that you know will bless their lives because they have told you about their favorite things.

**8 Subscription.** Since your volunteers do so much to feed the soul of the group, why not feed their souls? Get them a subscription to Moody Magazine, Discipleship Journal, Group, Jr. High Ministry, or a magazine of their choice. They might want to choose Discipleship Journal for their personal walk. Or they might choose Group to become more effective in youth work.

**9 Gift Book.** One of the favorites you may have asked for in #7 was a favorite author. Perhaps Max Lucado, Charles Swindoll, or Barbara Johnson? Wrap it and hand it to him or her over lunch.

**10 A Watch**. What better way to reward volunteers for their time than with a timepiece? Don't get a cheap watch that will turn green in about a month. Hold a youth group fundraiser and use the proceeds to purchase the watches. Include a note that says, "Thanks for all your help with getting the teens to the bus on time."

FIFTY TWO

# 10 Techniques for Building a Lasting Ministry

1 **Trust God to Produce the Fruit.** Discouragement enters when we feel the weight of every event. When we think we are the one who has to pull it off, we get overwhelmed. When we measure the ministry by attendance or new members we get dejected. A lasting ministry depends on God for the fruit. We can only do what He says and trust Him to do what He promised.



What are three promises that you need to remember and trust?

1.
2.
3.

2 **Remain Faithful.** Being faithful to God comes easily when everything runs smoothly, but what about the tough times? Do we find ourselves trying to escape our calling? Like Elijah, do we find ourselves hiding from our problems? Our work for God will last far beyond our lives when we stay faithful to the ministry even when it makes no sense.

3 **Keep the Finish in Focus.** At the beginning of each year thousands of people join a fitness center with visions of firm waistlines in mind. A few weeks later most of them drop out. Why? The progress didn't come fast enough.

The waistline didn't shrink fast enough. They forgot to focus on the finish, and only saw the immediate.

The apostle Paul said that he kept pressing toward the goal of Christ. He knew we don't attain spiritual maturity overnight. We can't expect to have all our ministry goals reached overnight either.

4 **Invest in People Not Programs.** Like gold and silver, programs perish. A hundred years from now youth conventions may cease to exist, but the soul will survive. Design your program to have an eternal impact. Use programs as a tool to reach people, not to overshadow them.

Each generation has its own formula that becomes the next big thing in church growth. We often think that we will be left behind if we don't get on board. If you know how to love and accept teenagers where they are, you will never be left behind.

5 **Develop Christ's Character.** Someone has defined character as what we are when no one is looking. Certainly it is what remains after all facades are stripped away. A unique aspect of Christ was that he remained the same all the time. That's character. When we develop integrity like that, our ministry will be remembered and continue to change lives even after we are dead. Sound impossible? Are we following a 2000-year-old carpenter?



6 **People Forget Messages, But They Remember Kindness.** If you don't mind a blow to the ego, ask your next class to list as many of your lessons as they can remember for the past six months. Next, ask them to write down anything someone said or did for them that was kind in the past six months. Which list do you think will be longer? Messages are great for the moment. Kindness is great forever.

7 **Prepare to Leave from the Beginning.** I was talking to a member of the San Antonio Church where Max Lucado serves and I asked, "What will happen to the church when Max leaves?" He replied, "Nothing. The church isn't build around Max, it's built around Christ. Max has led the church in a direction that is not dependent on

him." Lucado is prepared to leave even if he never leaves. His ministry has the long term mark of Jesus, not the short term mark of Max.

8 **Learn Balance.** There are workaholic ministers, playaholic ministers, and driftaholic ministers. We need balance to be successful. We don't have to be the perfect minister, perfect family member, and perfect whatever else. What we do need is a balanced life that is an example to others. If we are known for our hard work it may mean that we are ignoring our families. If we are known for our great tennis, it may indicate our lack of work ethic. A balanced life will point to symmetry in all areas.

9 **Love Much.** When Jesus ate with Simon, His host became disturbed when a sinful woman came in and anointed Jesus. Jesus saw the act as an expression of love. He then turned to Simon and explained the difference between him and the woman. Simon felt little need of forgiveness and loved little. The woman felt great need for forgiveness and loved much. Our ministries will flourish when we see ourselves in the greatest need of forgiveness and in turn we will be able to love much.

10 **Time is Relative.** It may take a lifetime for us to build a lasting ministry, or like Jesus, it may take three years. Whether or not our ministries last is dependent on Christ, not on time.

# Appendix A: The Spiritual Wheel

Have the teens grade themselves in different spiritual areas and assign a rating. "1" = poor, "10" = perfect. When they connect the dots the high points they circle are strengths, the low points are weaknesses. You can use the categories provided or develop your own.

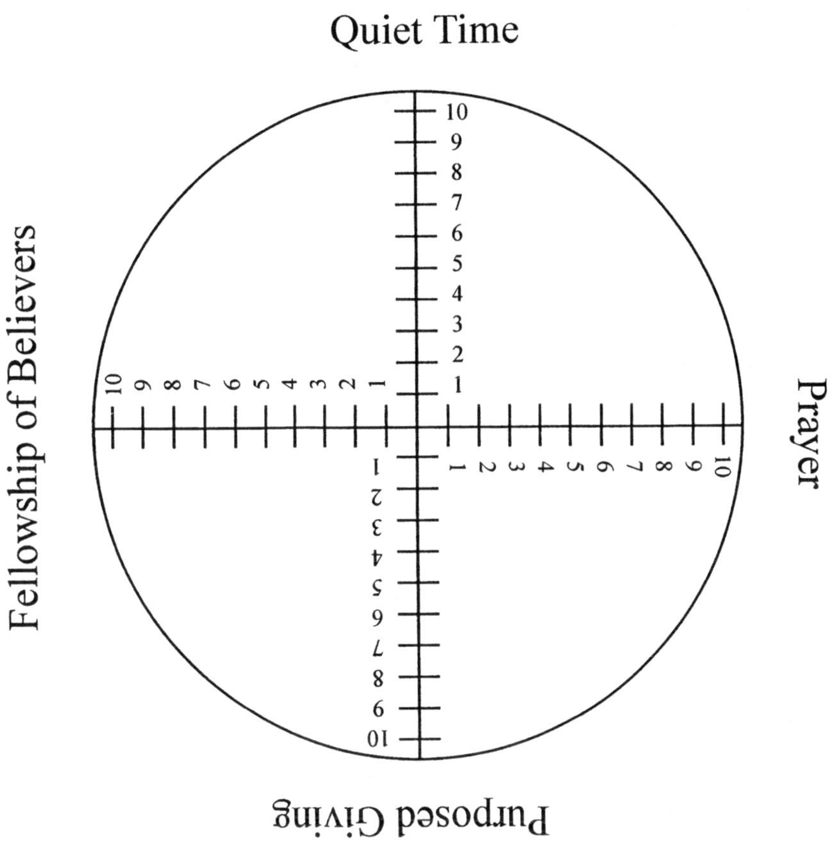

*10 X 50; 8.5" by 11"; 160 pages; $16.95*

**TIPS for:**

Recruiting Volunteers — Smart Goals
Leaving a Ministry — Personal Finances
Time Management

**TOOLS for:**

Boosting Creativity — Times of Crisis
Going Deep with God — Quiet Times
Affirming Teens

**TECHNIQUES for:**

Class Discussion — Counseling
Getting & Staying Fit — Family Time
Reaching Troubled Teens

*10 X 52; 8.5" by 11"; 176 pages; $16.95*

Get both books for only $29.95



Order Online: www.teenlifeministries.com
Plus get monthly encouragement and ministry tools at the Teen Life site.

*You Know You're a Youthworker If...*
*4" by 5.5", pages $4.95*

You know you're a Youthworker If..

- It was three months after you resigned that the congregation realized you were gone. And then only because they missed your wife and kids.
- Your family forgets your name by the end of the summer because they have seen you so little.

*You Know You're a Youthworker If...*

- Your hair has turned significantly gray by you thirtieth birthday.
- You have a burning desire to rebaptize select teens in shark infested waters.
- You've ever been asked, "Seriously, what do you do during the week."



# SLIDE-RULES

*Slide-Rules $2.00 each;*
*$1.75 for 100 or more*

There are two Slide-Rules available to get your group into the Word.

- **Life's Walk with Jesus** provides practical passages that deal 50 of the day to day pressures teens face. 150 passages.
- **Dating, Friendship, & Sexuality** provides scriptures on teen relationships. 50 topics. 150 passages.

How many times have you said to yourself, "I wish our group would turn to the Bible to answer their problems." Most Christian teens would look to God's word if they knew which ones would help. Pinpointing their needs in Scripture is difficult if they don't know where to begin.

Wouldn't it be great if something existed that would: 1) Help teens use God's Word as a life guide. 2) Serve as a quick and easy Bible reference tool. 3) Was inexpensive enough for every group member to be given one. 4) Was specifically designed for teens and their lives. 5) Could be carried anywhere. 6) Encouraged young people to discover God's answers for themselves instead of relying on "pat" answers?

Good questions, and Slide-rules are an easy answer. Think of Slide-rules as a teen-friendly concordance with the absence of fifty pounds.

The Leader's Guide takes you step by step through facilitating the sessions. Each chapter includes a letter written by a parent or adolescent that connects with the theme for the week. A thoroughly outlined lesson from God's word. Easy, yet powerful, in class exercises for families to participate in together. Exactly what the Family Journal includes concerning at home exercises, daily Bible study material, accountability journaling, and the weekly wrap-up. You also get promotional tools, and outreach ideas.

*Leader's Guide $29.95 available Fall 2000*

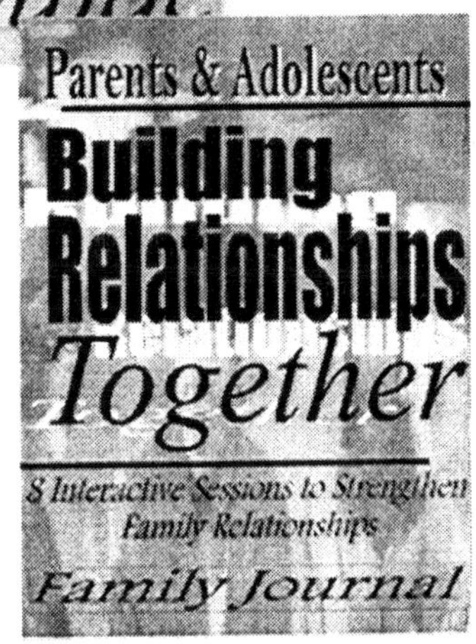


Each family member will use their personal Family Journal in class and home on a daily basis. This tool will promote learning during the sessions, self examination during personal development times, and foster interaction between family members during the Home Improvement sessions.

*Family Journal $9.95*

You've seen books and curriculum for parents, and books and curriculum for teens, but this study will allow them to work *together* while developing better relationships.

## That's Right! Your Families will actually be in the same class together!

Most materials on the market have parents in one class learning how to "handle" their children. While the young people go into another class that teaches them how to "get along with" their parents. Parents & Adolescents: Building Our Relationships Together allows families to work, yep, *together*!

### 8 Critical Themes:

Week 1: Commitment to God and Family
Week 2: A Spiritual Home Under Construction
Week 3: Communication
Week 4: Love, the Bond of Perfection.
Week 5: It's Our Decision
Week 6: Understanding One Another's Needs
Week 7: Defusing Fights, feuds, and Arguments
Week 8: Praise, Honor, and Appreciation

**Coming Fall 2000**

Soft Knocks Open Big Doors; 150 pages
$9.95

Tired of beating on the heart of God? Do your fists ache? Are your knuckles raw? Do you wonder just how hard you have to pound to get His attention?

Maybe it's time to stop banging and start trusting.

Trust Him to hear your quiet voice in the middle of a hectic day.

Trust Him to answer a whispered prayer on a crowded highway.

Trust Him to invite you to enter His joy regardless of the circumstances.

Discover that a soft knock on the
heart of God
opens big doors.

*Devotional/inspirational reading*

Audio Tape & 12 page workbook,
$9.95

**ONE:** Step by Step to Unforgettable Messages. Learn how to craft a lesson that will leave teens remembering, not revolting.

## ORDER INFORMATION

Online: www.teenlifeministries.com
Phone: 334-277-7726
Email: tlm@teenlifeministries.com
Mail: Teen Life Ministries
3009 Willow Lane Dr
Montgomery, AL 36109

| Item # | Description | Qty. | Price | Subtotal |
|---|---|---|---|---|
| | | | | |
| | | | | |
| | | | | |
| | | | | |
| | | | | |
| | | | | |

Shipping:
Up to $20..........$3.20
$21-50.............$4.90
$51-$100..........$8.30
$100 and up.......$12.80

Order total: ________

Tax:8% AL Res. only ________

Shipping: ________

Total: ________

Name

Church

Address

City, St, Zip

email

Phone

Method of Payment

- ☐ Check
- ☐ Visa
- ☐ MasterCard
- ☐ American Express

Credit Card #

Exp. date

Signature X

174

For information about other Teen Life Products call or write us at:

Teen Life Ministries
3009 Willow Lane Dr
Montgomery, AL 36109
(334)277-7726

Or visiti us online:

www.TeenLifeMinistries.com
TLM@teenlifeministries.com